BEST OF
CROSBY, STILLS & NASH

Cover photo by Henry Diltz

Music transcriptions by Pete Billmann, Jeff Jacobson, Paul Pappas and Jeff Story

ISBN 0-634-05921-1

7777 W. BLUEMOUND RD. P.O. BOX 13819 MILWAUKEE, WI 53213

Visit Hal Leonard Online at
www.halleonard.com

Carry Me

Words and Music by David Crosby

Drop D tuning, Capo II:
(low to high) D-A-D-G-B-E

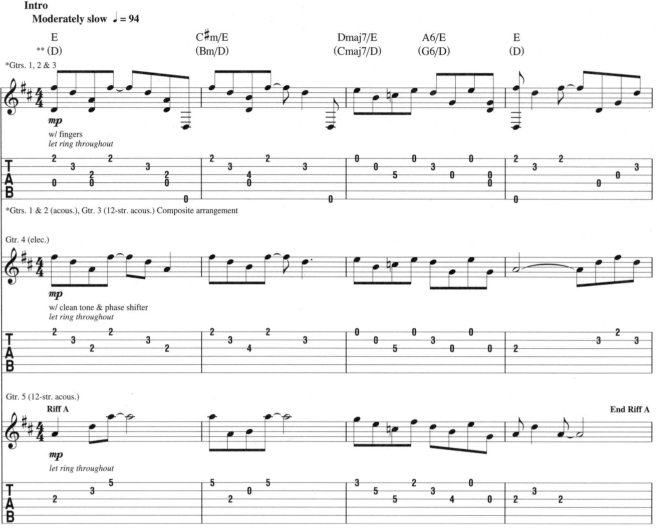

*Symbols in parentheses represent chord names respective to capoed guitar.
Symbols above reflect actual sounding chords (implied harmony). Capoed fret is "0" in tab.

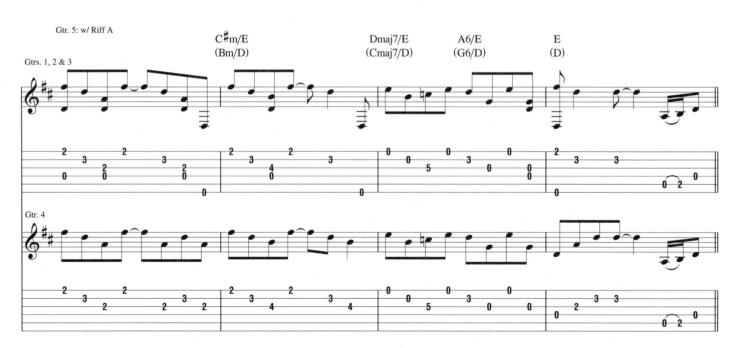

1. When I was a young man I found an old dream.

Was as bat-tered and worn a one

as you have __ ev - er seen. _____ Now I made it some

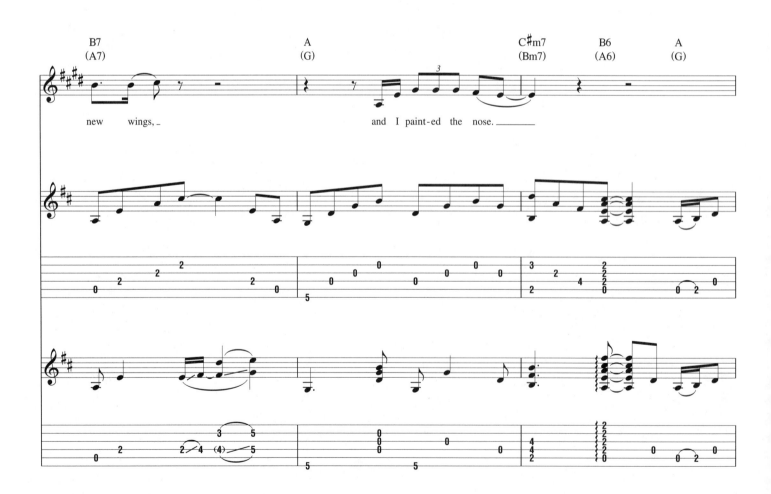

new wings, _ and I paint-ed the nose. _____

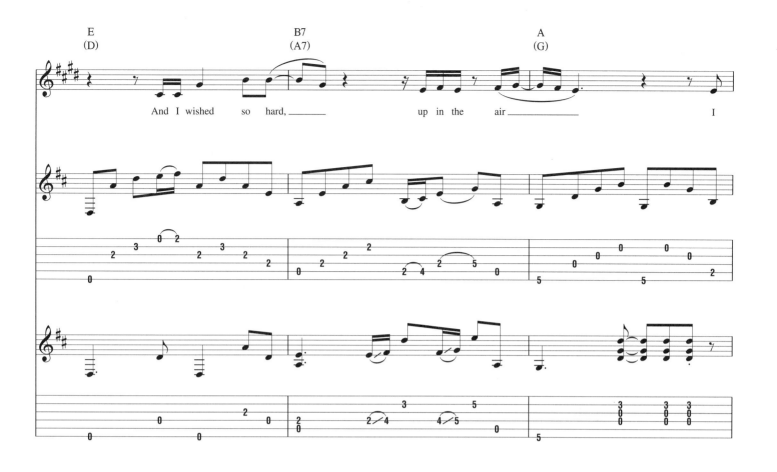

E
(D)

B7
(A7)

A
(G)

And I wished so hard, _____ up in the air _____ I

Chorus

C#m B A
(Bm) (A) (G)

E
(D)

C#m/E
(Bm/D)

ro - ose ____ sing - ing, ____ "Car - ry me, _____ car - ry me, ____ yeah.
(Car - ry me, car - ry me.

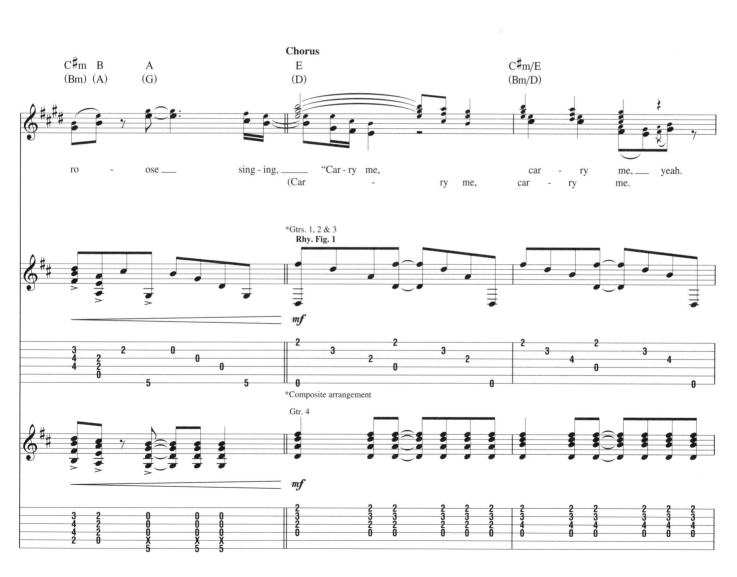

*Gtrs. 1, 2 & 3
Rhy. Fig. 1

*Composite arrangement

Gtr. 4

5

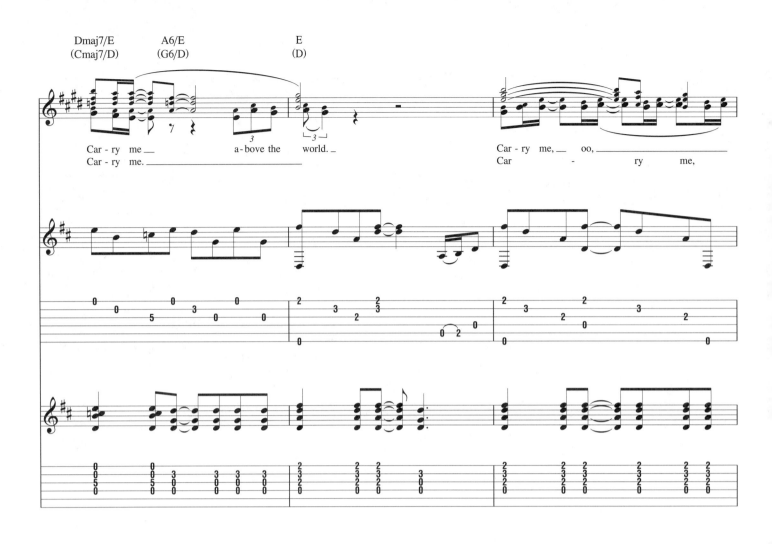

Car - ry me ___ a-bove the world. ___ Car - ry me, ___ oo, ___

Car - ry me. ___ Car - ry me,

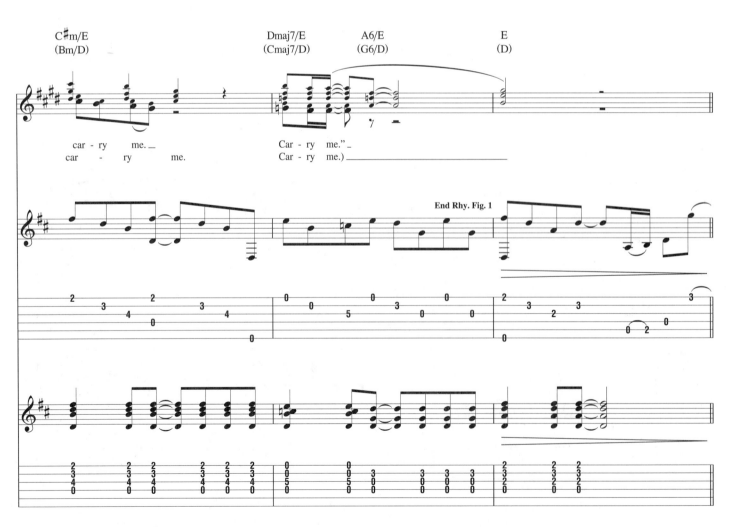

car - ry me. ___ Car - ry me." ___

car - ry me. Car - ry me.) ___

End Rhy. Fig. 1

Verse

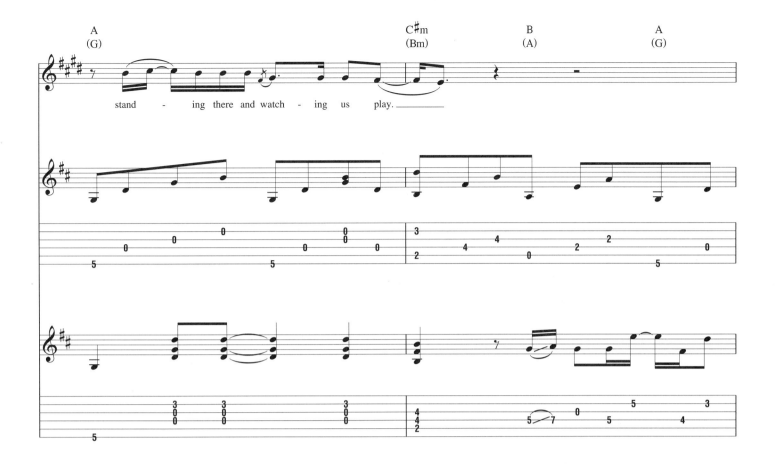

stand - ing there and watch - ing us play. _____

For a while __ there __ the mu -

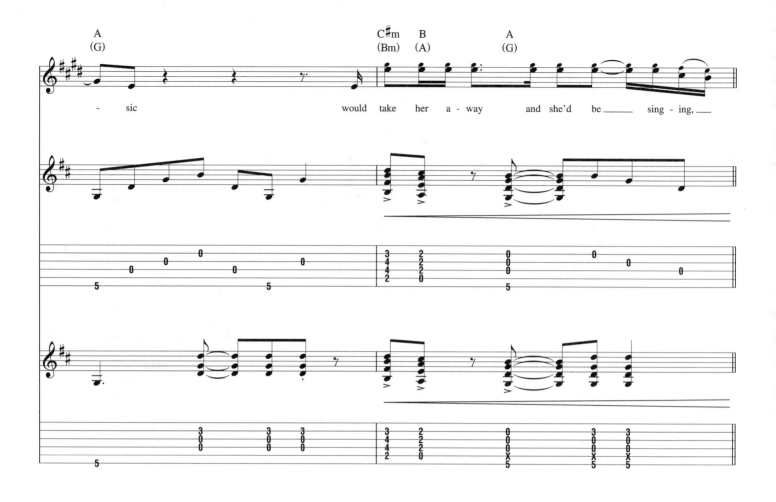

would take her a - way and she'd be _____ sing - ing, _____

Chorus

Gtrs. 1, 2 & 3: w/ Rhy. Fig. 1

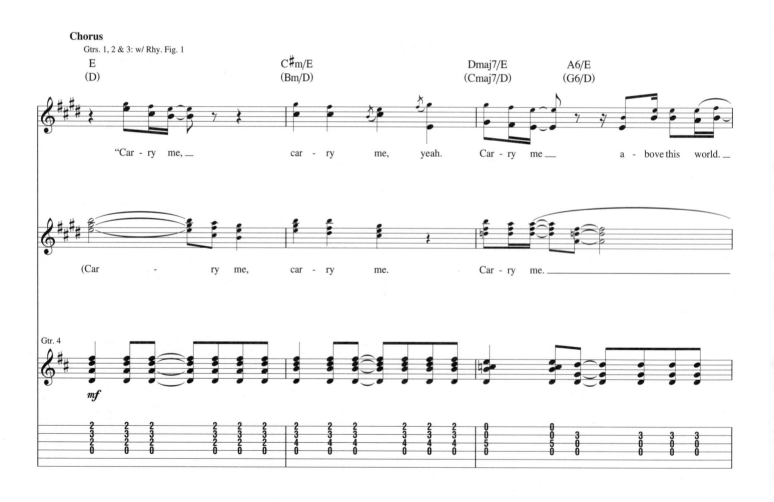

"Car - ry me, _____ car - ry me, yeah. Car - ry me _____ a - bove this world. _____

(Car - ry me, car - ry me. Car - ry me. _____

Gtr. 4

mf

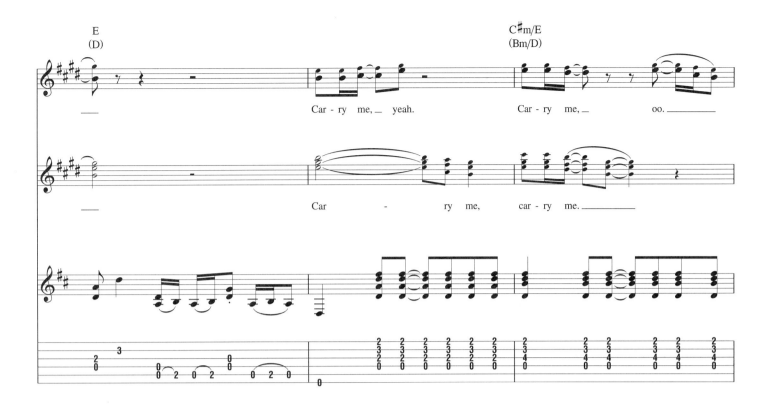

*Composite arrangement

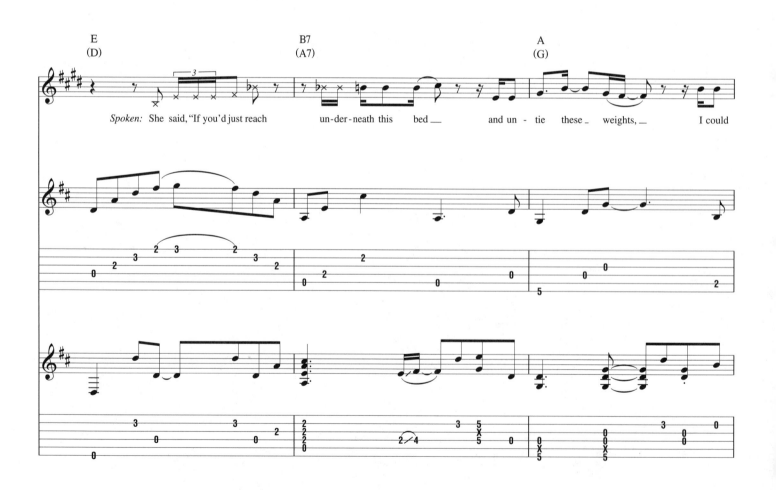

sure - ly fly." _____ She's still __ smil - ing, but she's tired. _____

She'd like to hear _ that last bell ring. _____ You know if she still

Chorus

14

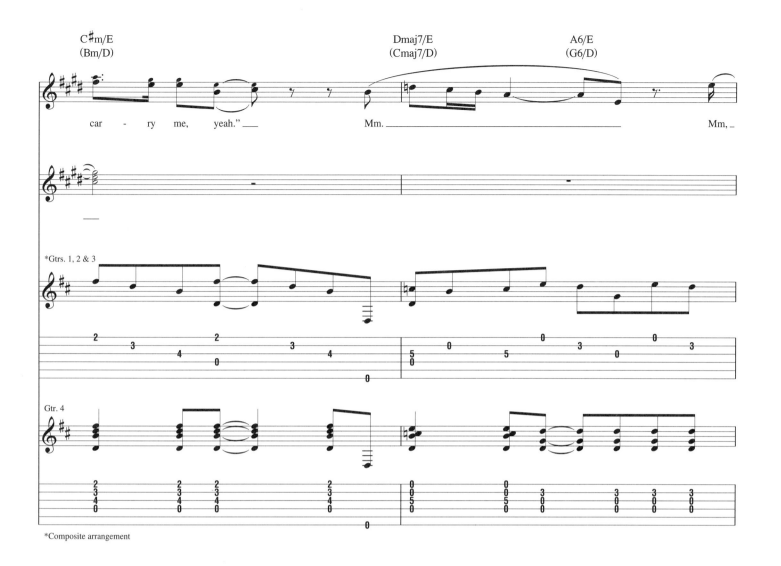

*Composite arrangement

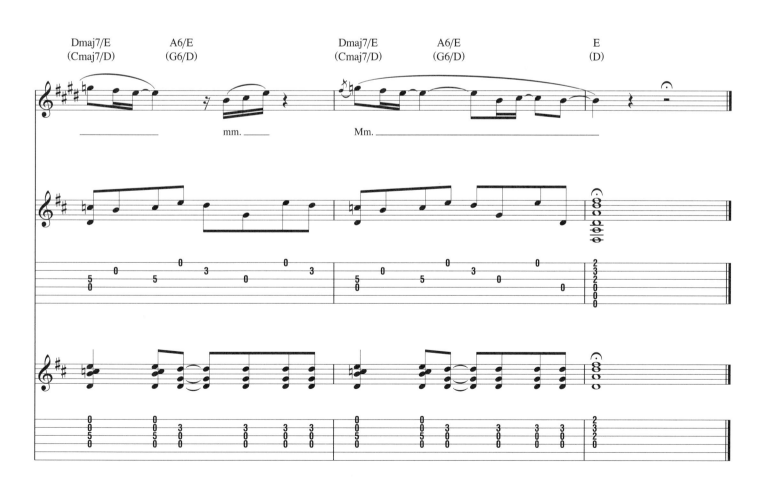

from *Déjà Vu*
Carry On
Words and Music by Stephen Stills

Gtr. 1: Open E5 tuning, down 1/2 step:
(low to high) E♭-E♭-+-E♭-E♭-B♭-E♭

Gtrs. 2-5: Tune down 1/2 step:
(low to high) E♭-A♭-D♭-G♭-B♭-E♭

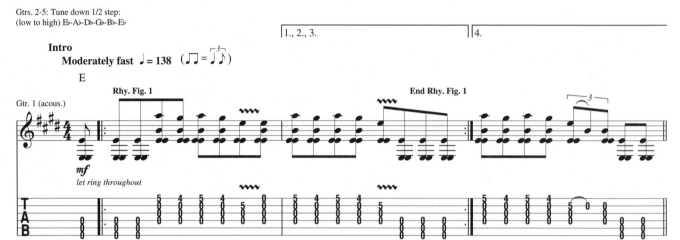

Intro
Moderately fast ♩ = 138

Verse

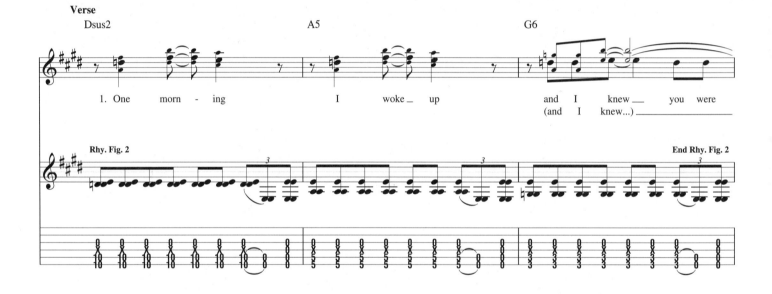

1. One morn-ing I woke up and I knew you were
(and I knew...)

re-al-ly gone. A new day, a new way,

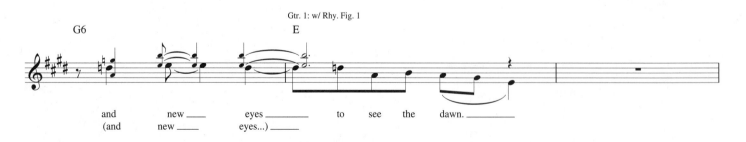

and new eyes to see the dawn.
(and new eyes...)

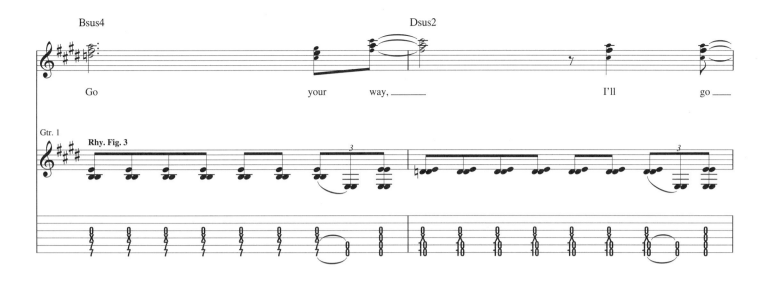

Bsus4   Dsus2

Go   your way, _____   I'll   go _____

Gtr. 1

Rhy. Fig. 3

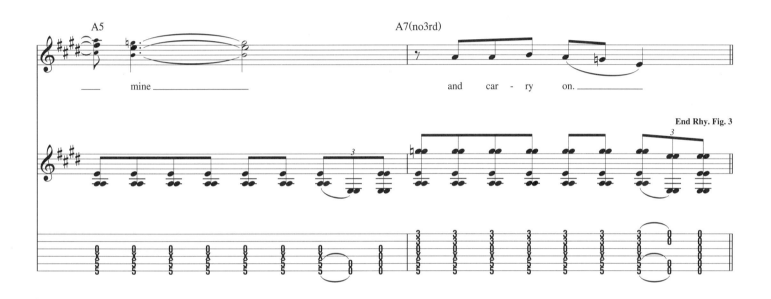

A5   A7(no3rd)

_____ mine _____   and   car - ry   on. _____

End Rhy. Fig. 3

Interlude

Gtr. 1: w/ Rhy. Fig. 1 (2 times)

E

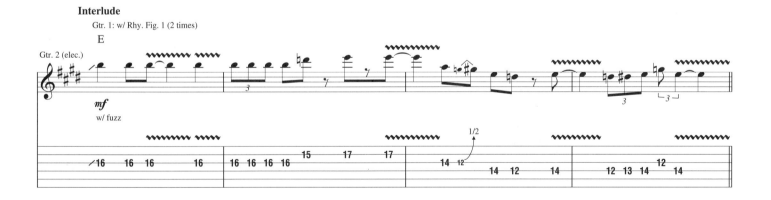

Gtr. 2 (elec.)

mf

w/ fuzz

1/2

Verse

Gtr. 1: w/ Rhy. Fig. 2
Gtr. 2 tacet

Dsus2   A5   G6

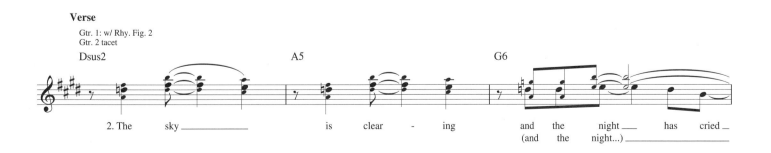

2. The   sky _____   is   clear - ing   and   the   night _____ has   cried _____
                                             (and   the   night...) _____

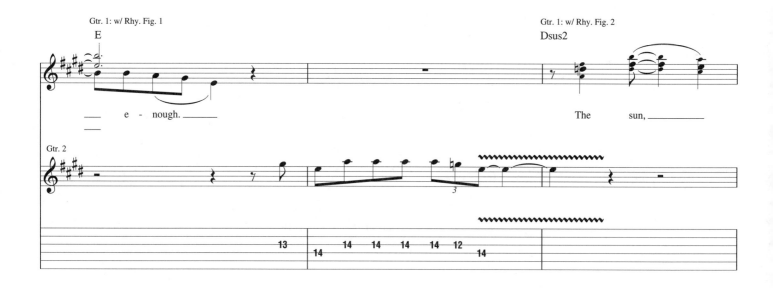

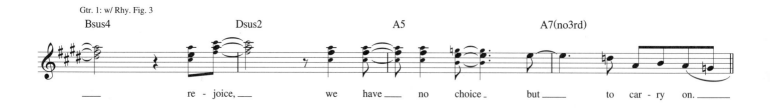

Interlude

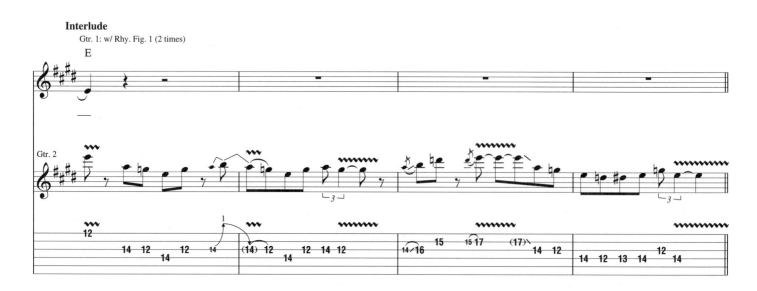

Verse

Gtr. 1: w/ Rhy. Fig. 2

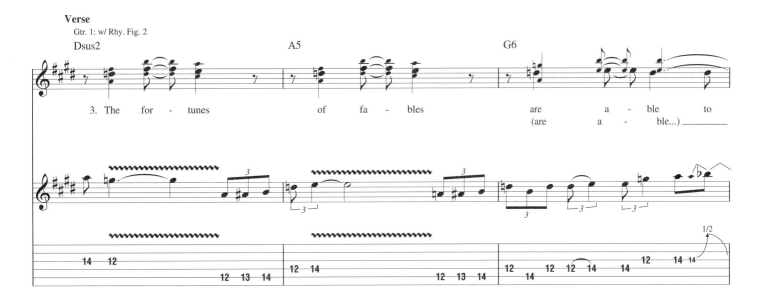

3. The for - tunes of fa - bles are a - ble to
(are a - ble...)

Gtr. 1: w/ Rhy. Fig. 1   Gtr. 1: w/ Rhy. Fig. 2

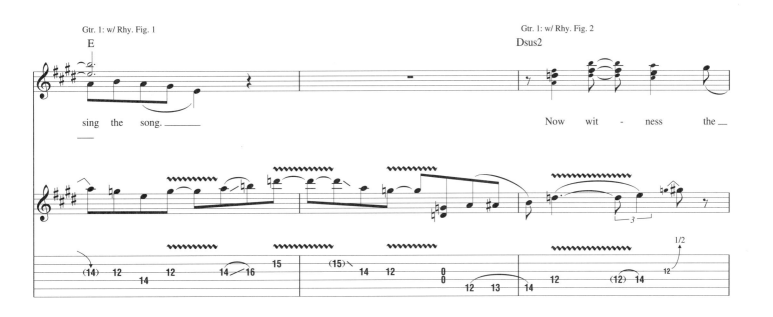

sing the song. Now wit - ness the

Gtr. 1: w/ Rhy. Fig. 1

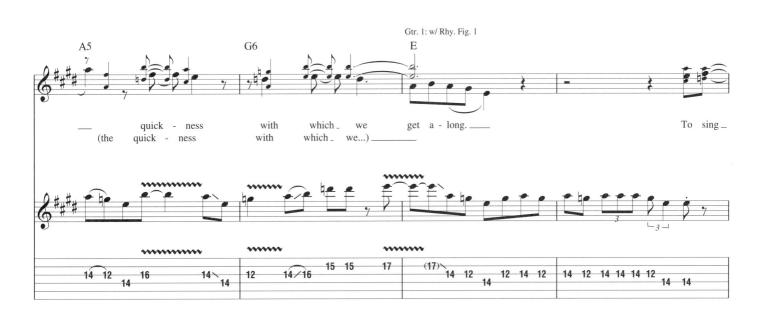

quick - ness with which we get a - long. To sing
(the quick - ness with which we...)

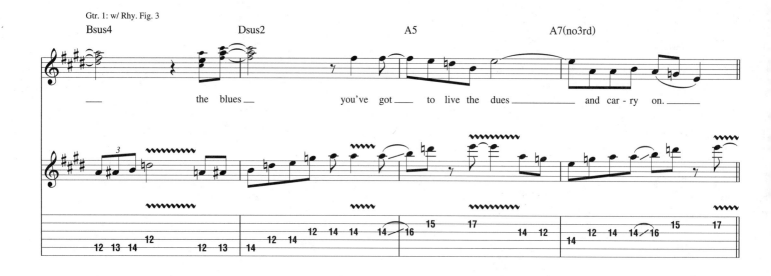

the blues ___ you've got ___ to live the dues ___ and car - ry on. ___

Interlude

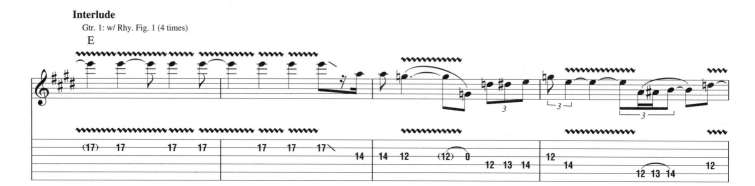

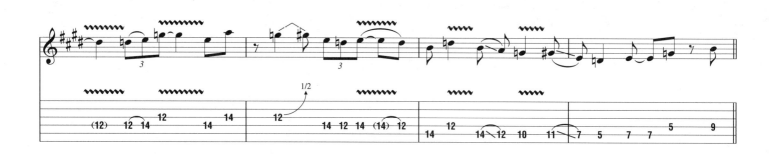

Bridge

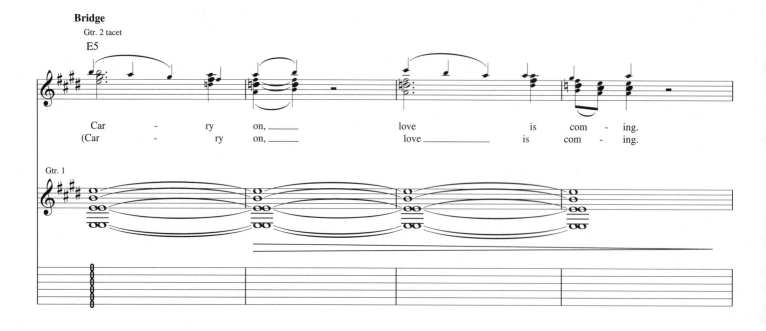

Car - ry on, ___ love is com - ing.
(Car - ry on, ___ love ___ is com - ing.

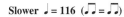

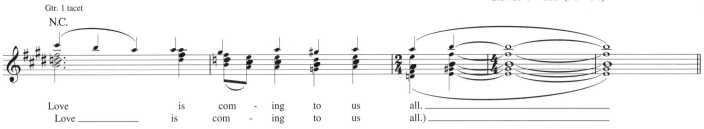

Love   is   com -   ing   to   us   all. _____
Love _____ is   com -   ing   to   us   all.) _____

Organ Solo

*Organ arr. for gtr.

Guitar Solo

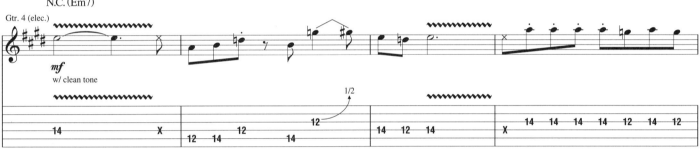

Outro-Guitar Solo

Gtr. 3: w/ Riff A (till end)
Gtr. 4 tacet

N.C. (Em7)

Begin fade

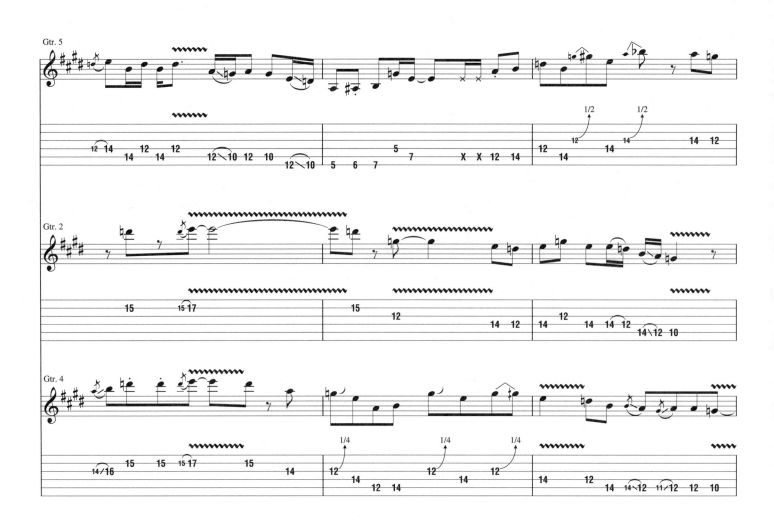

Fade out

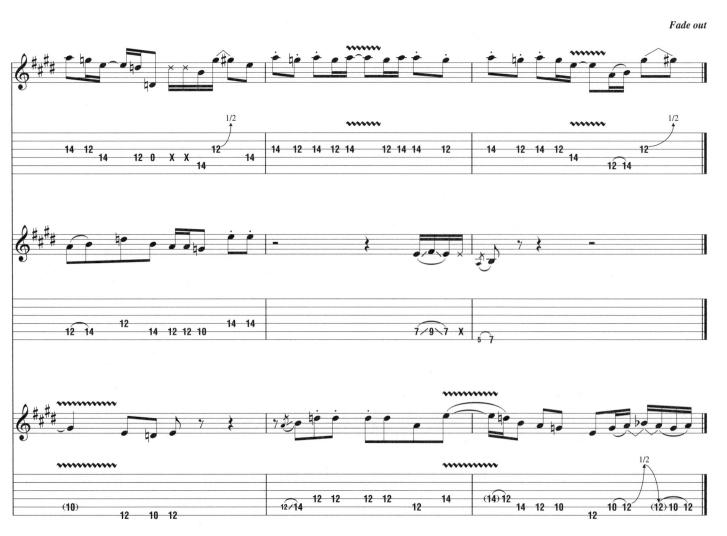

from *Carry On*

Change Partners

Words and Music by Stephen Stills

*If 24 frets are not available, substitute harmonic for upper note.

**If 24 frets are not available, substitute harmonic for lower note.

from *Carry On*

Chicago

Words and Music by Graham Nash

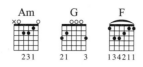

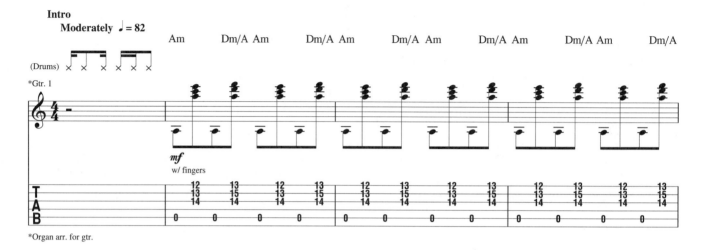

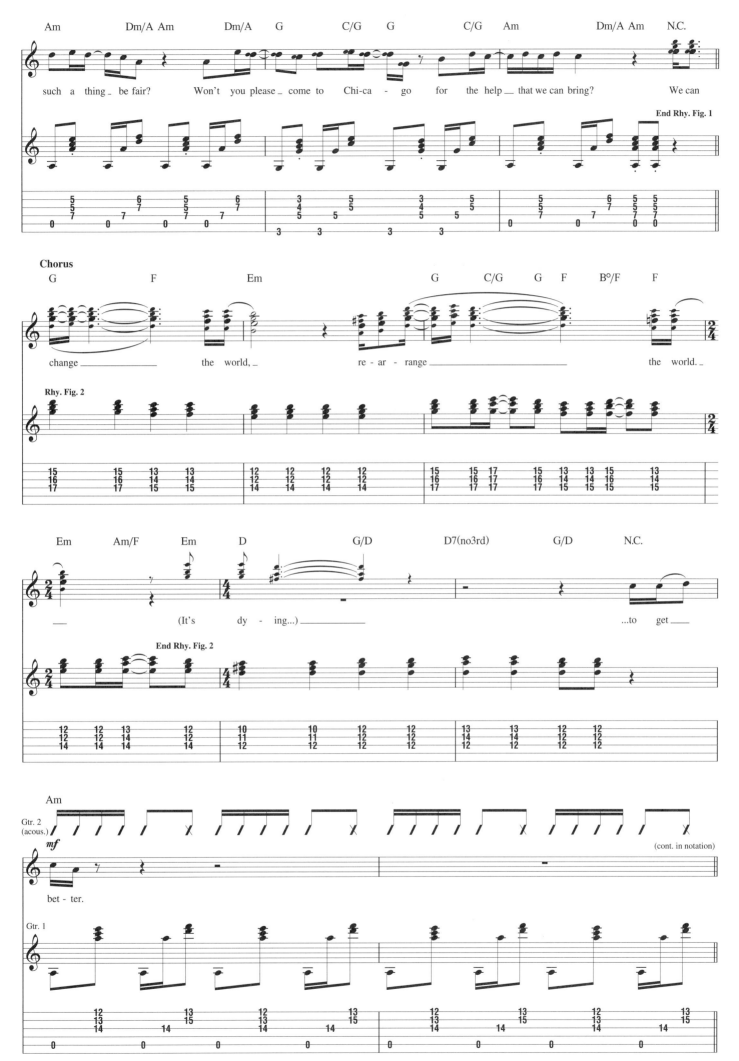

Verse

*Chord symbols reflect overall harmony.

2. Pol - i - ti - cians, sit ___ your-selves down, there's noth-ing for you here. ___ Won't you please ___
3. Some-how peo - ple must ___ be free, I hope the day ___ comes ___ soon. Won't you please ___

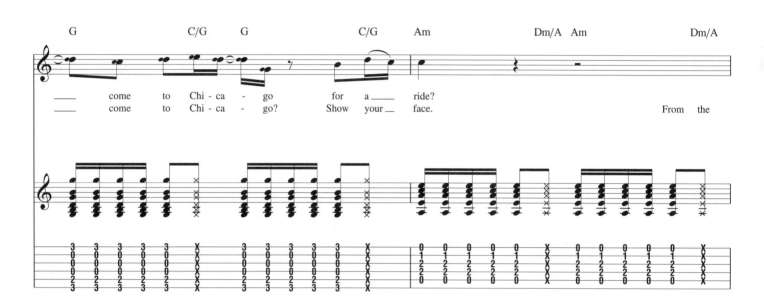

___ come to Chi - ca - go for a ___ ride?
___ come to Chi - ca - go? Show your ___ face. From the

Don't ask Jack ___ to help ___ you 'cause he'll turn the oth - er ear. Won't you please ___
bot - tom of ___ the o - cean to the moun - tains of ___ the moon. ___ Won't you please ___

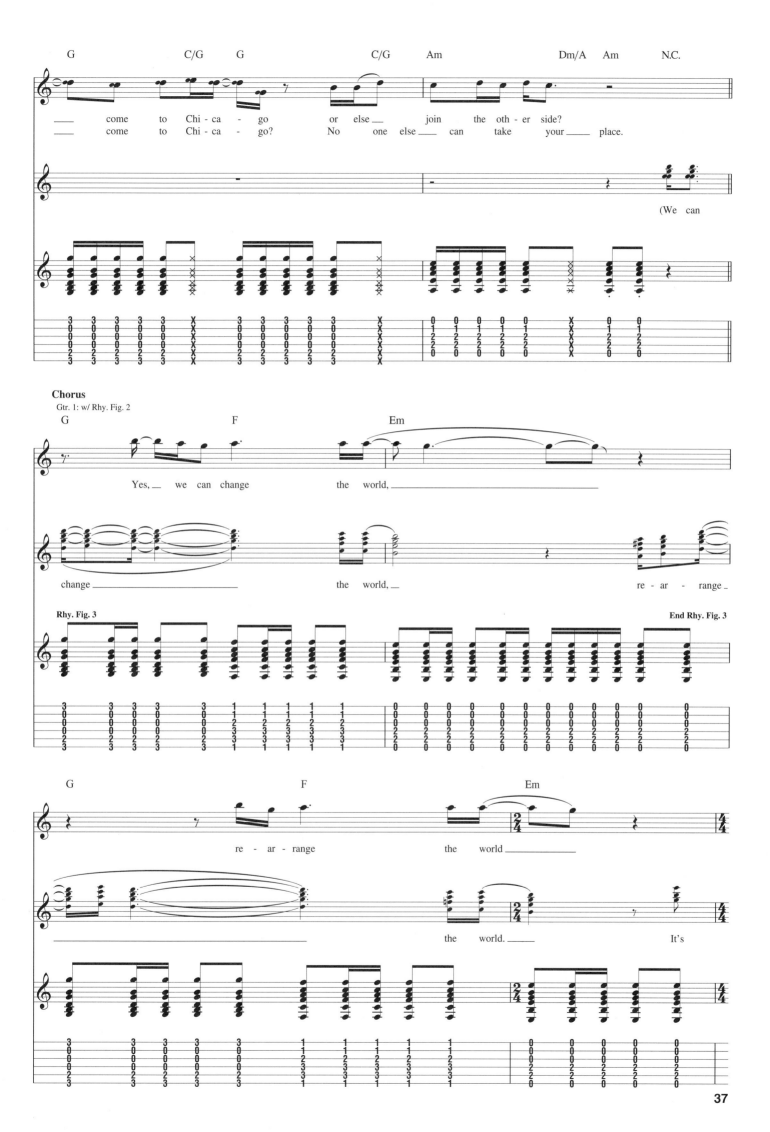

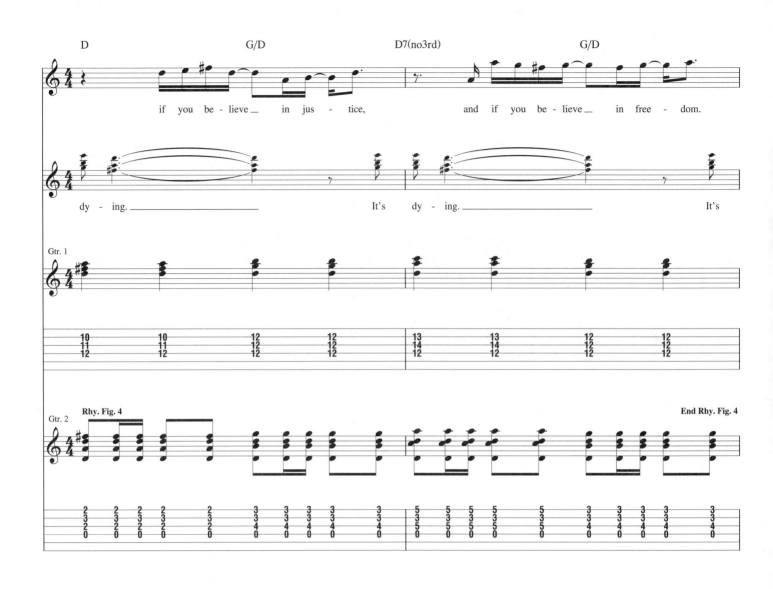

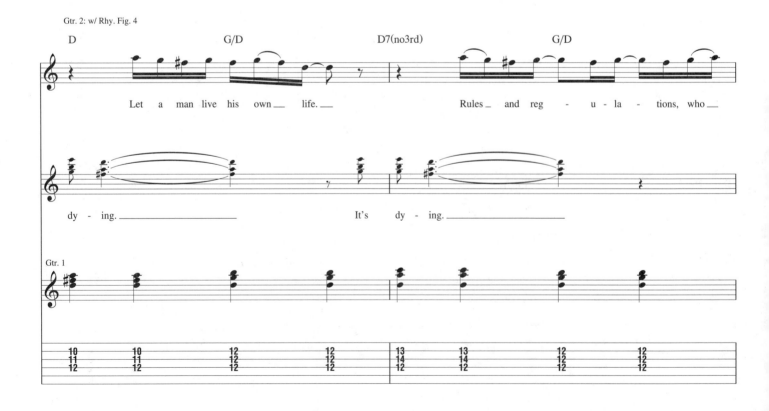

Outro

from *CSN*

Dark Star

Words and Music by Stephen Stills

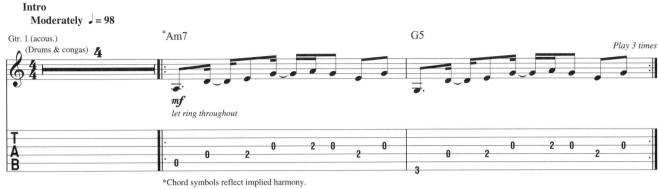

*Chord symbols reflect implied harmony.

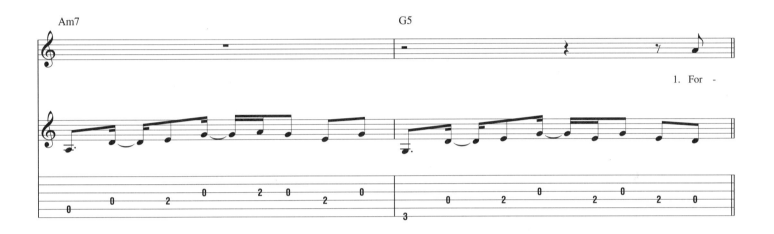

Verse

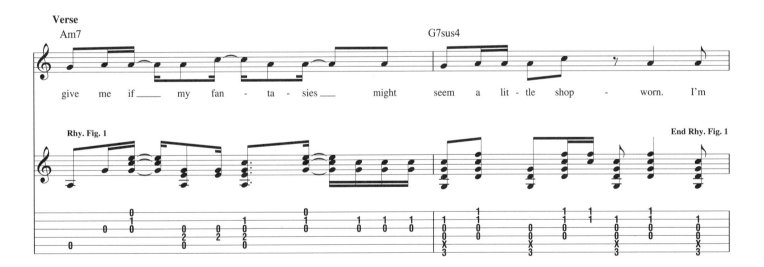

give me if ___ my fan - ta - sies ___ might seem a lit - tle shop - worn. I'm

sure you've heard ___ it all ___ be - fore. I won - der what's ___ the right form. ___

Love songs writ-ten for ___ you, it's been go-ing down ___ for years. ___ But to

sing what's in ___ my heart ___ seems more hon-est than the tears. ___ I am

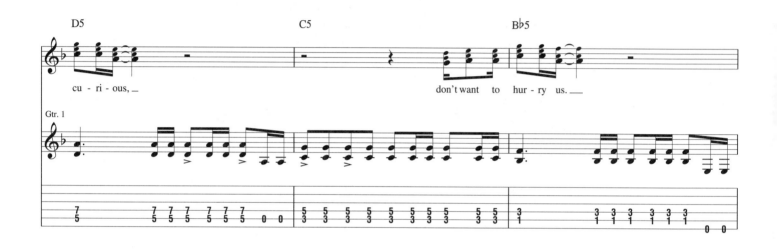

cu - ri - ous, ___ don't want to hur - ry us. ___

Gtr. 1

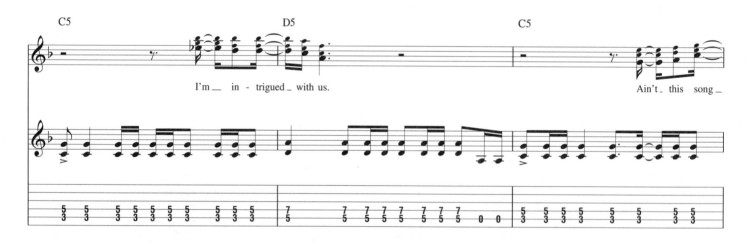

I'm ___ in - trigued ___ with us. Ain't ___ this song ___

___ a bust? I don't care, ___ Dark Star.

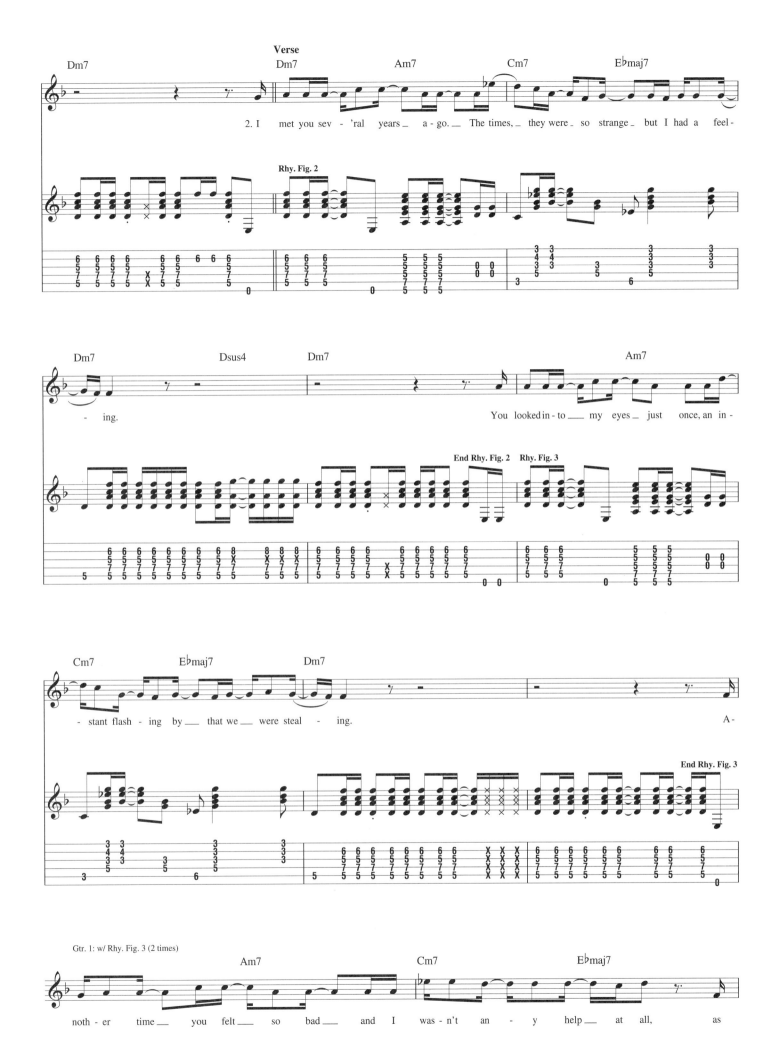

I re - call.___

We did - n't know___ quite what___ to do, so we

left the want - ing be ___ still ___ there for me and you. ___

𝄋 **Chorus**

Gtr. 1: w/ Rhy. Fig. 4 (2 times)

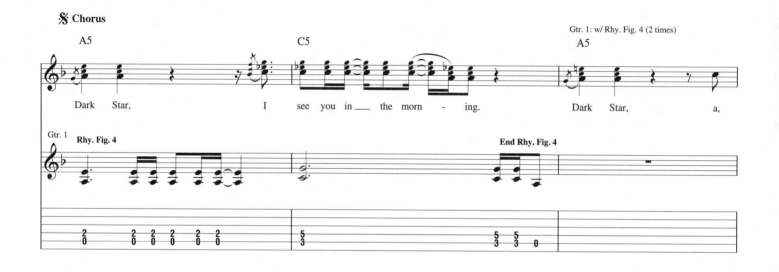

Dark Star,   I see you in ___ the morn - ing.   Dark Star,   a,

Gtr. 1   Rhy. Fig. 4   End Rhy. Fig. 4

sleep - in' next ___ to me. ___   Dark Star,   let the mem - 'ry of ___ the eve - ning be the

To Coda 1 ⊕

To Coda 2 ⊕

first thing that you think ___ of when you o - pen up ___ your smile ___ and see me, Dark Star.

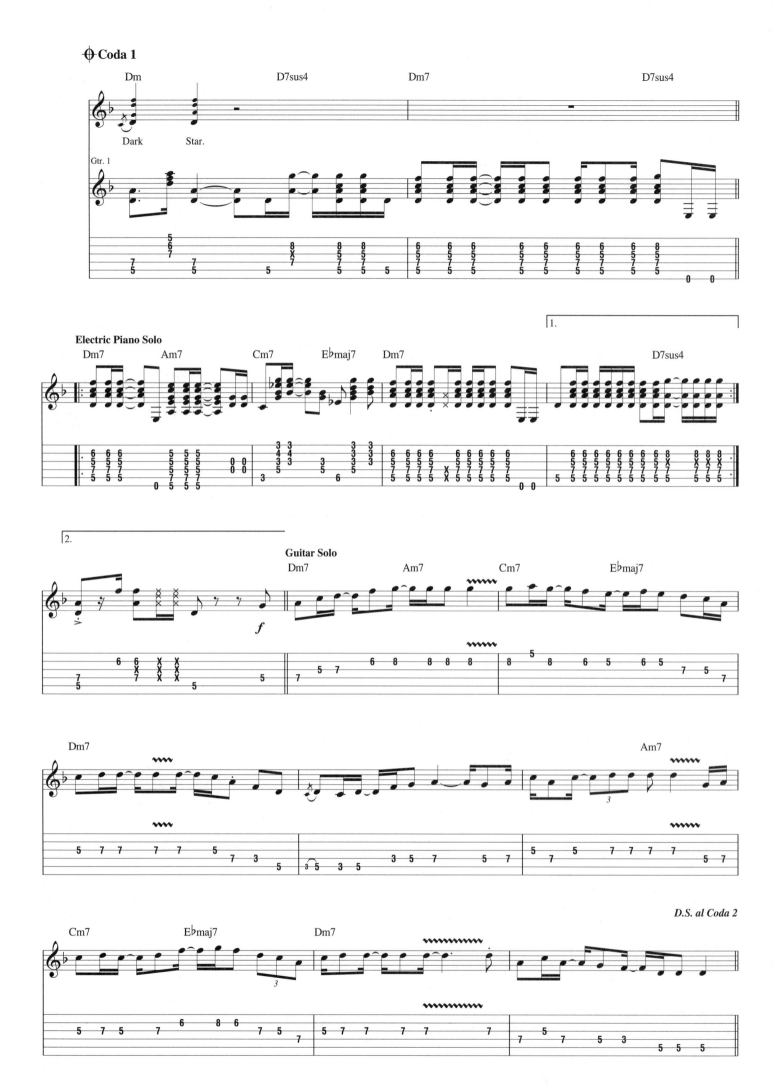

Coda 2

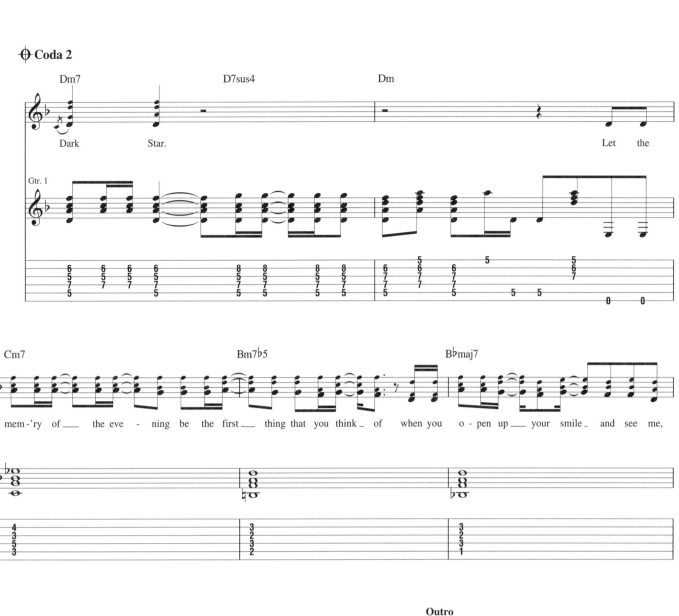

Dark Star.

Let the

mem-'ry of ___ the eve - ning be the first ___ thing that you think ___ of when you o - pen up ___ your smile ___ and see me,

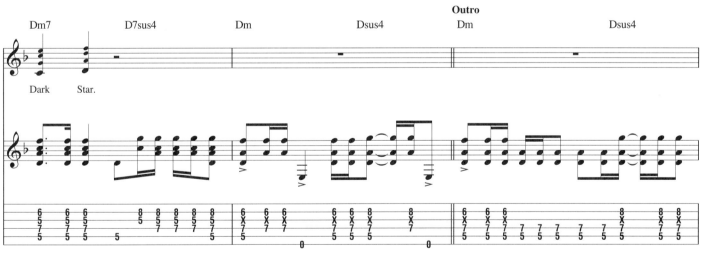

Outro

Dark Star.

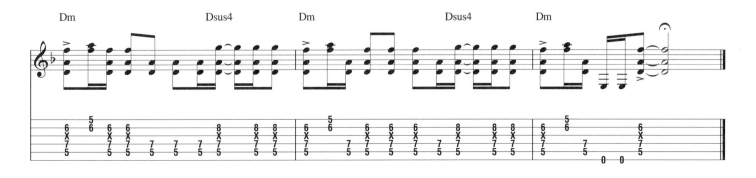

from *Déjà Vu*

Déjà Vu

Words and Music by David Crosby

Gtrs. 1 & 2, Open Em11 tuning:
(low to high) E-B-D-G-A-D

Gtr. 5, Drop D tuning:
(low to high) D-A-D-G-B-E

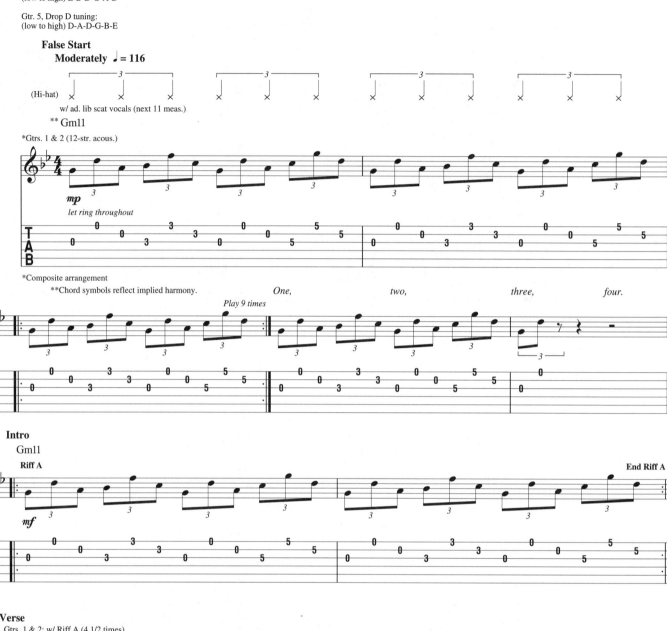

*Composite arrangement
**Chord symbols reflect implied harmony.

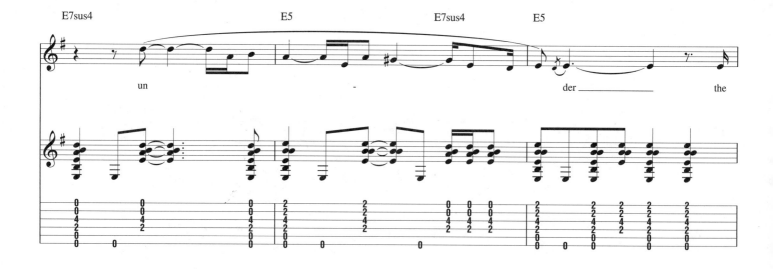

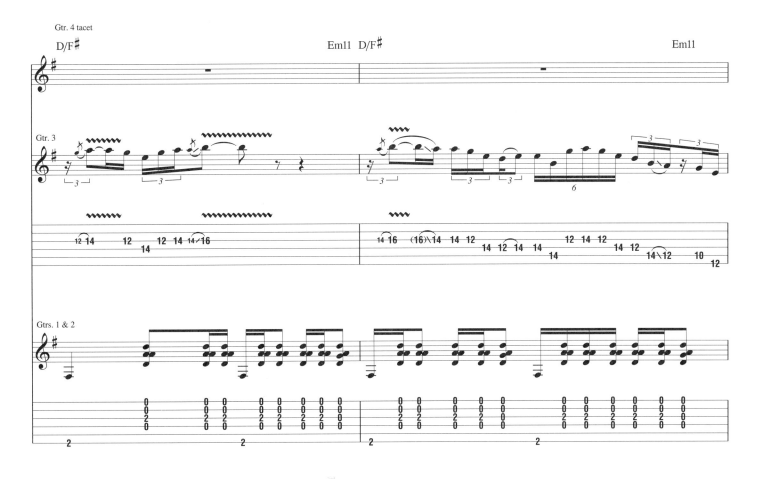

Outro

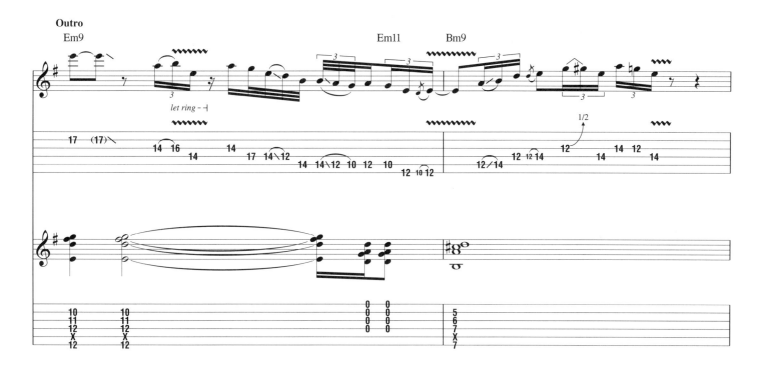

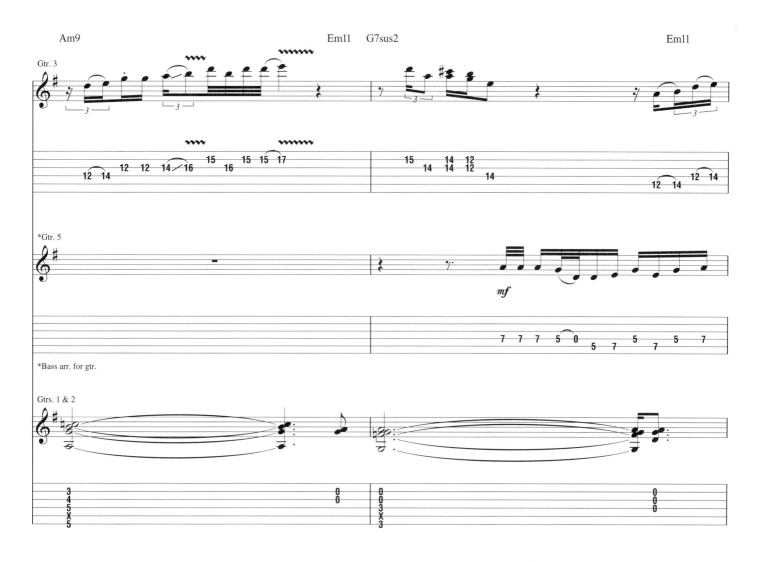

Voc. Fig. 1

End Voc. Fig. 1

(We have all ___ been here ___ be - fore.   We   have all ___ been here ___ be-fore.)

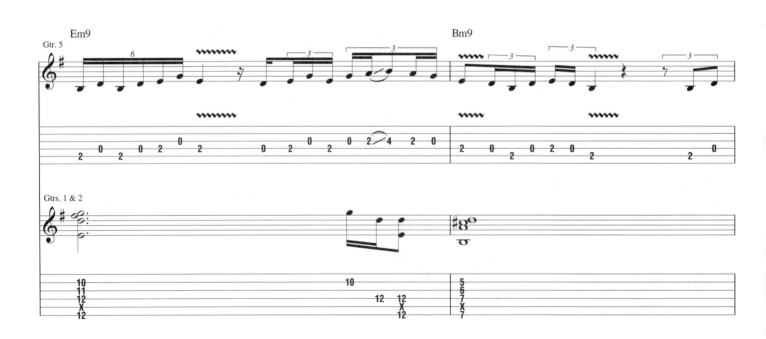

Em9

Bm9

Gtr. 5

Gtrs. 1 & 2

G7sus2

Em11

(We have all ___ been here ___ be - fore.

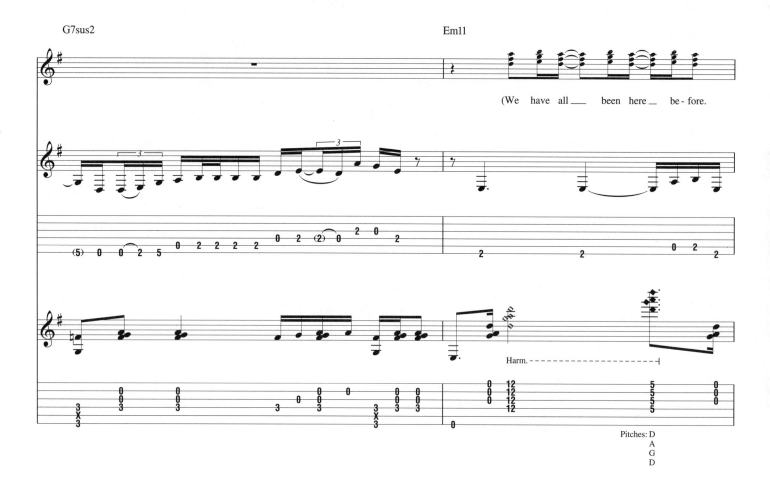

Pitches: D
A
G
D

Em9

Bm9

We have all ___ been here ___ be - fore.) ___

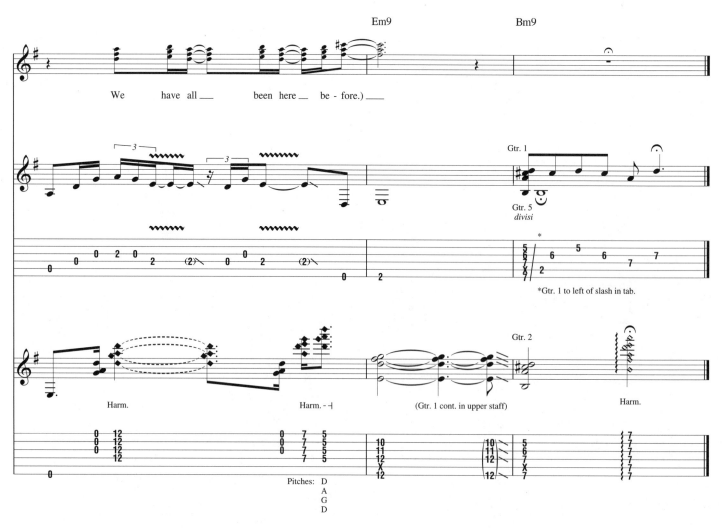

*Gtr. 1 to left of slash in tab.

Pitches: D
A
G
D

from *American Dream*

Got It Made

Words and Music by Stephen Stills and Neil Young

*Chord symbols reflect overall harmony.

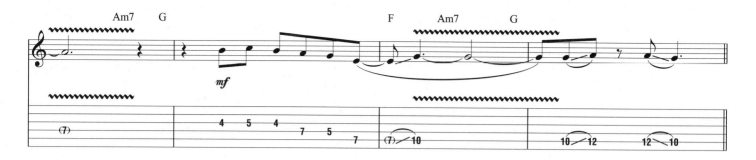

Bridge

When you came __ to save the world, __ I caused your dreams __ to fade. __
(When you __ came. __

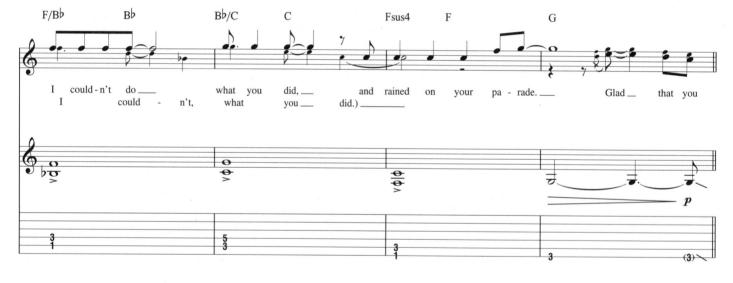

I could-n't do __ what you did, __ and rained on your pa-rade. __ Glad __ that you
I could-n't, what you __ did.) __

Interlude

got it made. __

*w/ tone control rolled back (next 7 meas.)

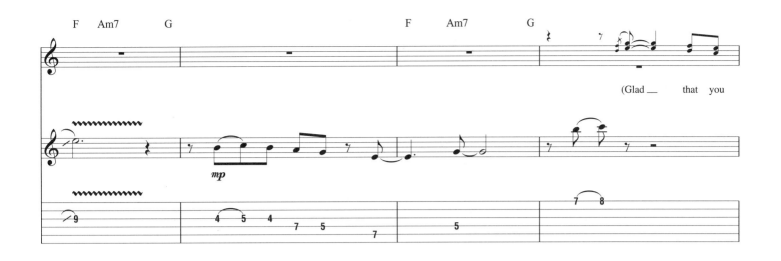

(Glad ___ that you

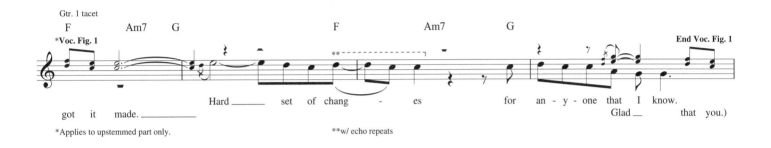

Gtr. 1 tacet

*Voc. Fig. 1   End Voc. Fig. 1

Hard ___ set of chang - es   for an - y - one that I know.
got it made. ___   Glad ___ that you.)

*Applies to upstemmed part only.   **w/ echo repeats

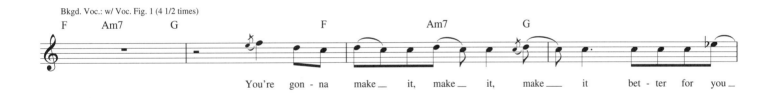

Bkgd. Voc.: w/ Voc. Fig. 1 (4 1/2 times)

You're gon - na make ___ it, make ___ it, make ___ it bet - ter for you ___

___ and me and an - y - one else you know.   Just don't for - get ___ me.

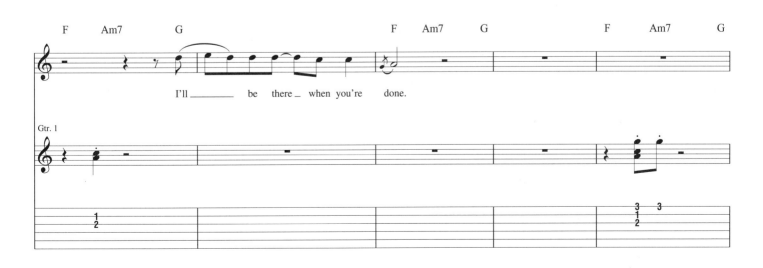

I'll ___ be there ___ when you're done.

Gtr. 1

from *Crosby, Stills & Nash*

Guinnevere

Words and Music by David Crosby

Open Em11 tuning:
(low to high) E-B-D-G-A-D

Intro
Moderately ♩ = 116

*Em11

Gtrs. 1 (12-str. elec.)
& 2 (acous.)

mf
w/ fingers
let ring throughout

*Chord symbols reflect implied harmony.

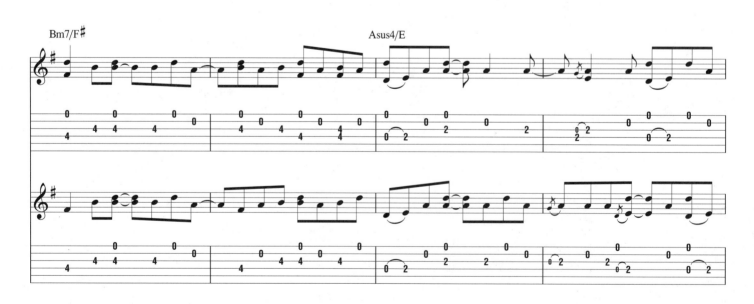

Em13

*Gtrs. 1 & 2

Rhy. Fig. 1

End Rhy. Fig. 1

*Composite arrangement

Verse

Em13

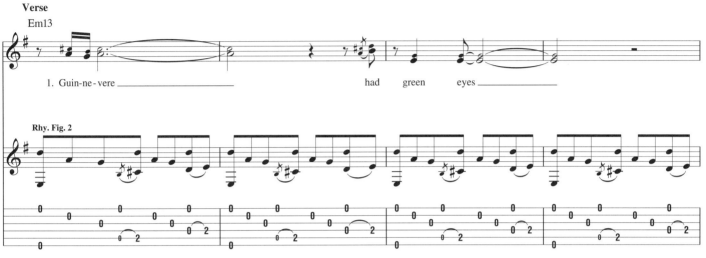

Rhy. Fig. 2

1. Guin-ne-vere _____ had green eyes _____

like yours, _____ mi' la - dy, like _____ yours. _____

Gm11	Gm11/F	Gm11/E	Gm11/D	Gm11

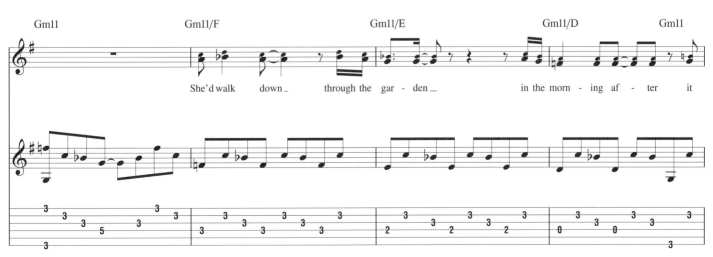

She'd walk down _ through the gar - den _ in the morn - ing af - ter it

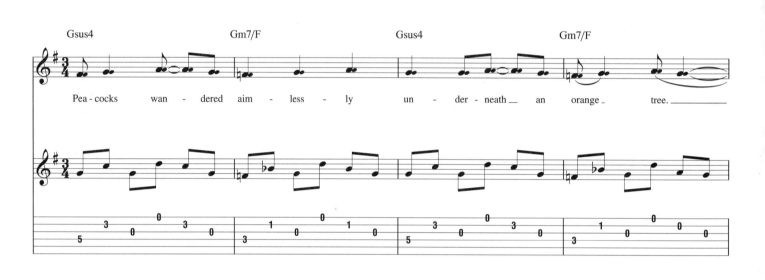

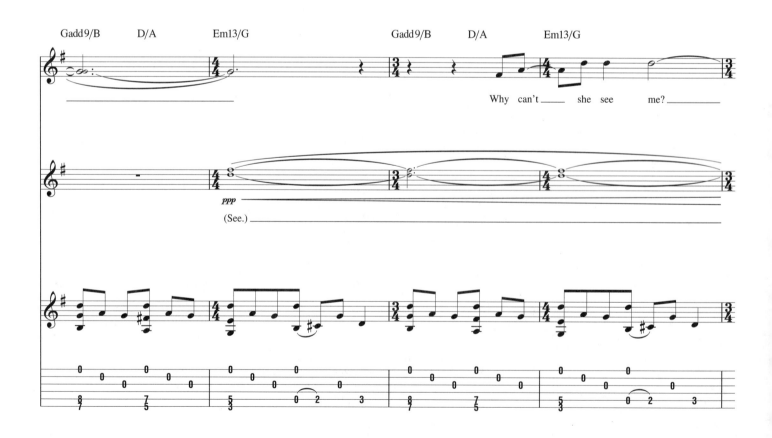

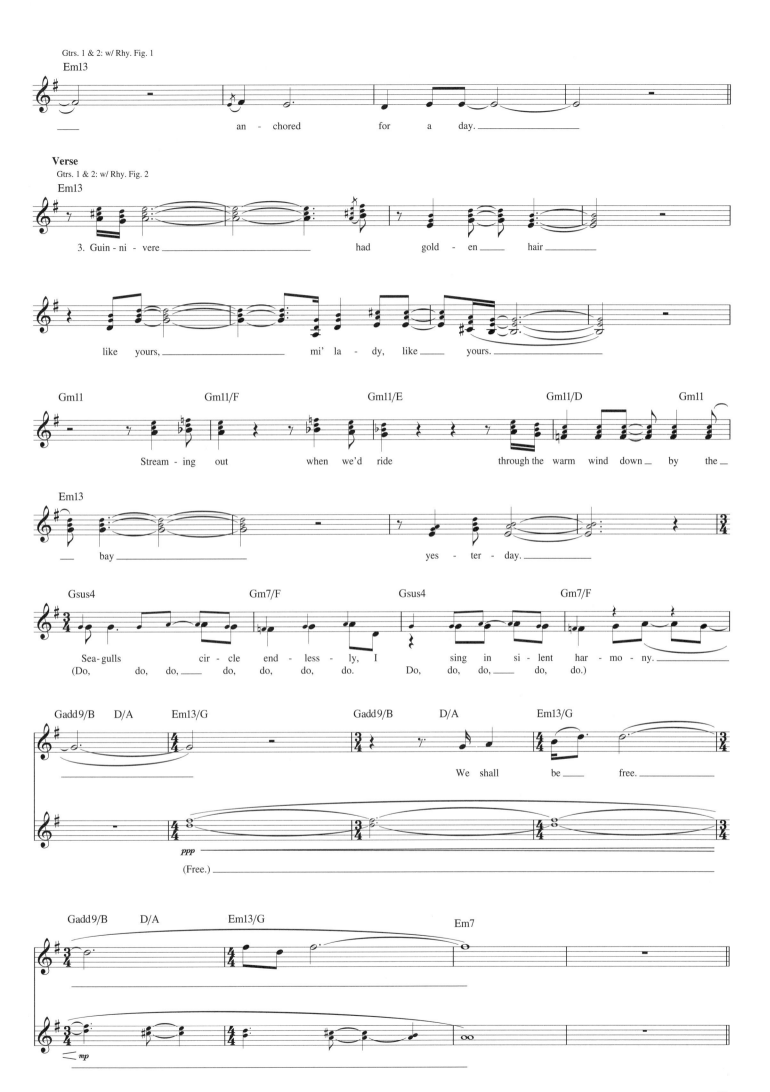

Outro

Em11

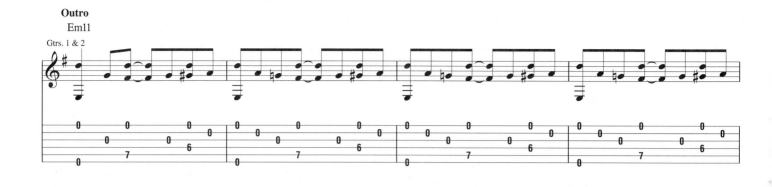

Bm9   Bm11   Bm9   Gadd9

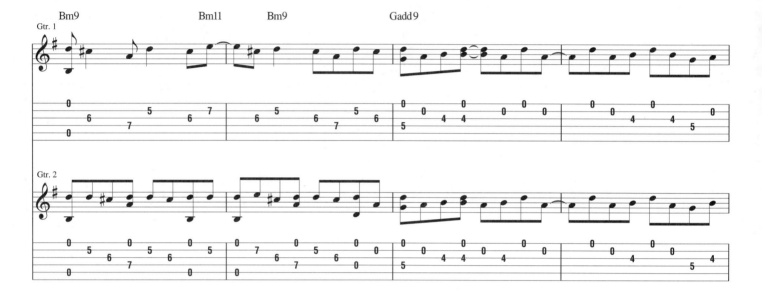

Bm7/F#   Asus4/E

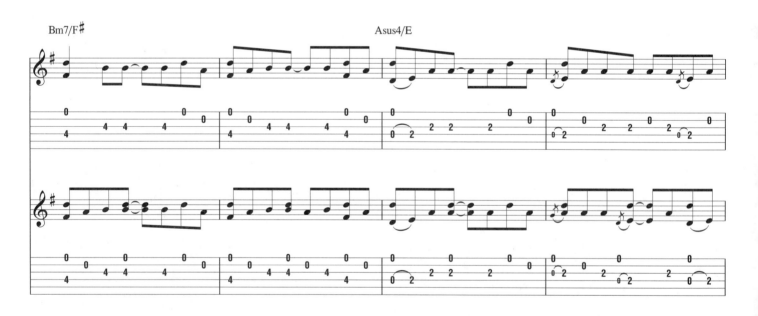

Repeat and fade

Em13

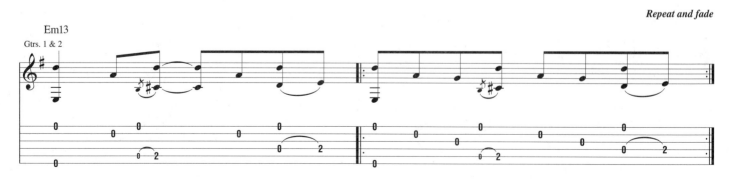

70

from *Crosby, Stills & Nash*

Helplessly Hoping

Words and Music by Stephen Stills

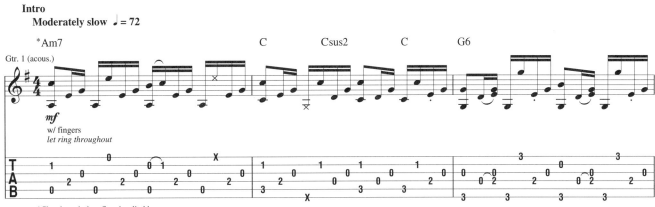

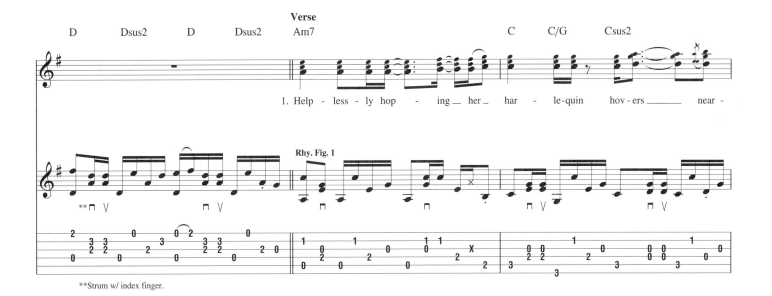

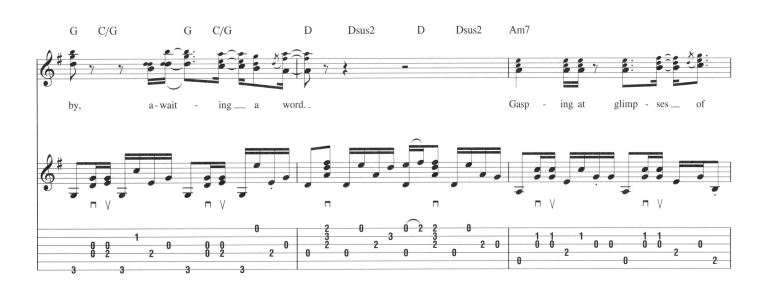

gen - tle ___ true spir-it, he runs, wish - ing he ___ could fly - y, on - ly to

trip ___ at the sound ___ of ___ good - bye - ye - ye. ___

End Rhy. Fig. 1

Verse
Gtr. 1: w/ Rhy. Fig. 1

2. Word - less - ly watch - ing, ___ he ___ waits by the win - dow ___ and won - ders at the emp - ty place ___ in - side.

___ Heart - less - ly help - ing ___ him - self to her bad ___ dreams, he wor -

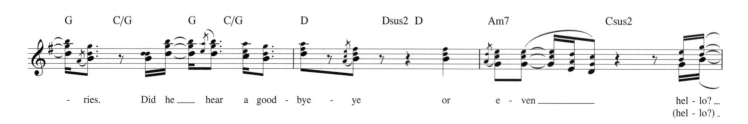

- ries. Did he ___ hear a good - bye - ye or e - ven _____ hel - lo?
(hel - lo?)

73

in a la-dy who lin-gers say-ing she __ is lo-

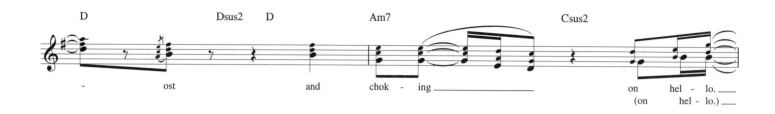

-ost and chok-ing __ on hel-lo.
(on hel-lo.) __

Chorus

__ They are one __ per-son. They are two __ a-lo-o-ne. They are three __

Gtr. 1

__ to-geth-er. They are for - or each oth-er.

Just a Song Before I Go

Words and Music by Graham Nash

Traveling twice _ the speed _ of sound, _ it's eas - y to _ get burned. _
Driving me to _ the air - port _ and to the friend - ly skies. _

When the shows _ were o - ver, _ we had to get _ back home. _ And
Going through se - cu - ri - ty, I held her for _ so long. _ She

when we o - pened up the door, I had to be a - lone.
fi - n'lly looked _ at me

2. She ___ in love, ___ and she was gone.

Guitar Solo

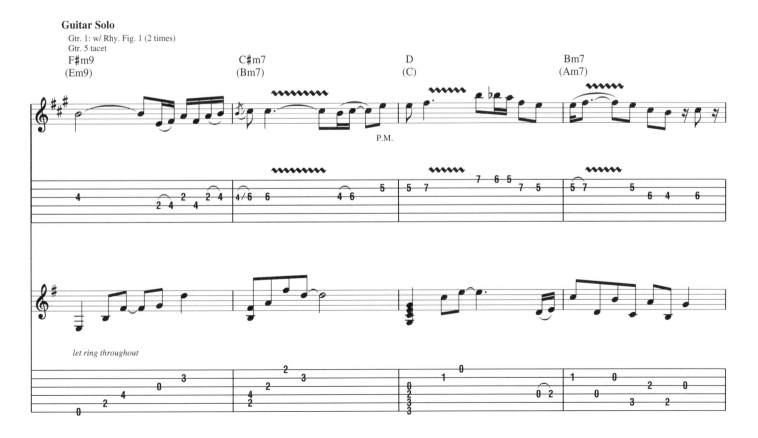

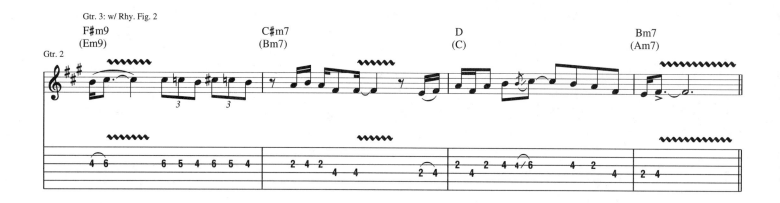

Outro-Verse

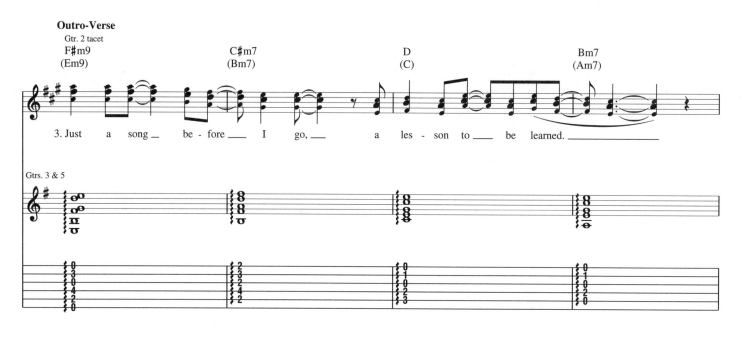

3. Just a song be-fore I go, a les-son to be learned.

Trav-el-ing twice the speed of sound, it's eas-y to get burned.

from *Crosby, Stills & Nash*
Long Time Gone
Words and Music by David Crosby

Intro
Moderately ♩ = 104

*Chord symbols reflect overall harmony.

Verse

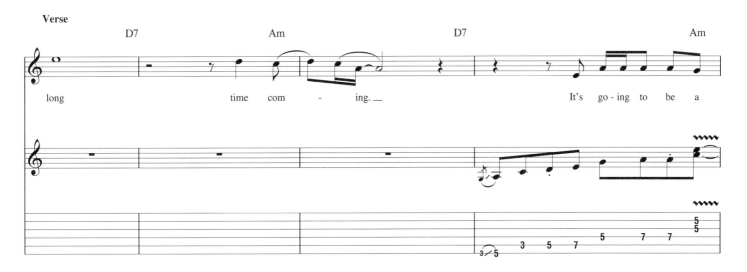

Chorus

Gtr. 1: w/ Rhy. Fig. 1

Interlude

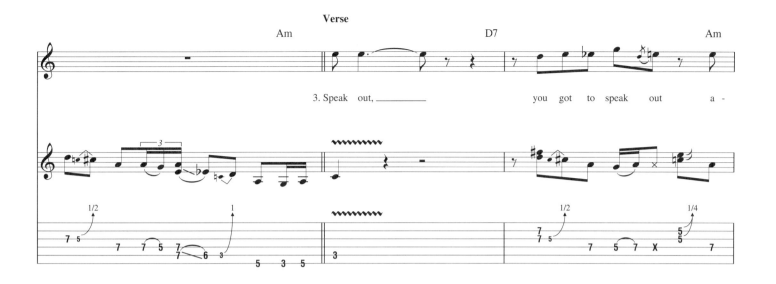

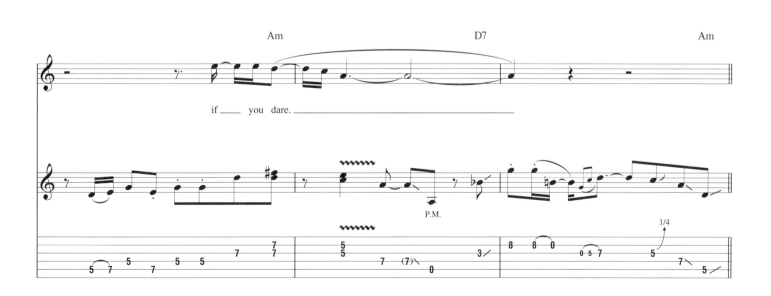

Interlude

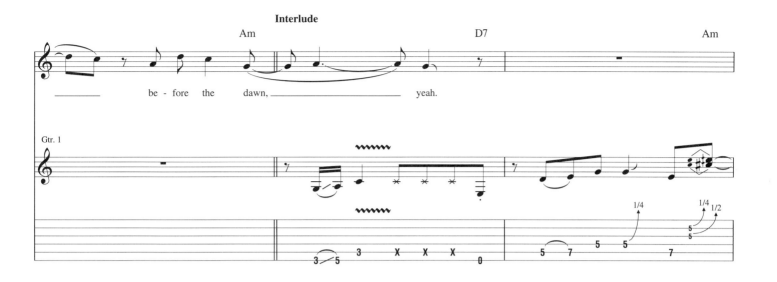

be - fore the dawn, _____ yeah.

Gtr. 1

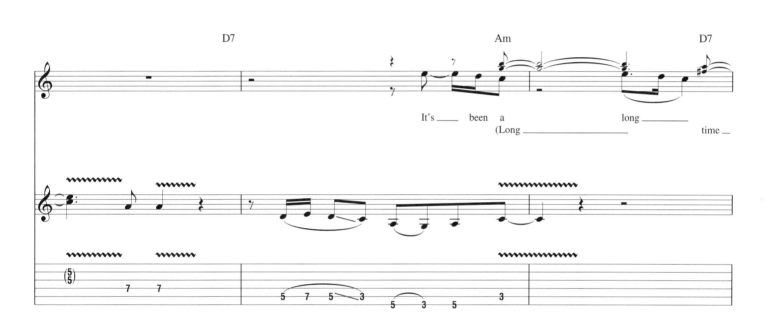

It's _____ been a _____ long _____
(Long _____ time _

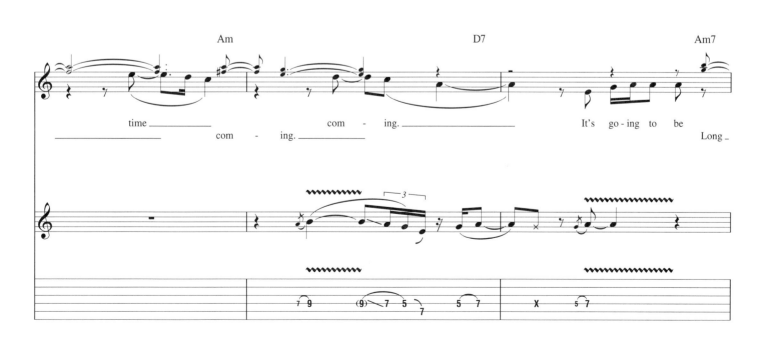

time _____ com - ing. _____
_____ com - ing. _____ It's go - ing to be
Long _

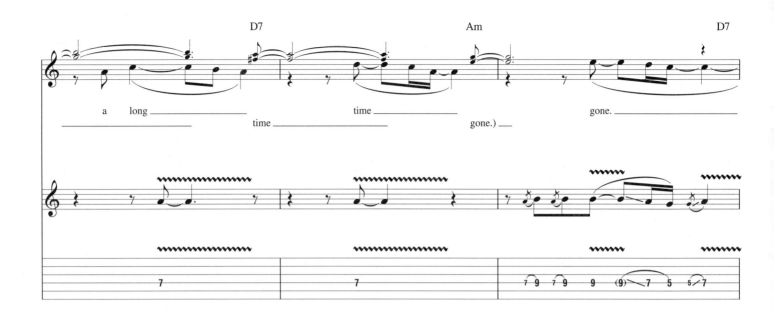

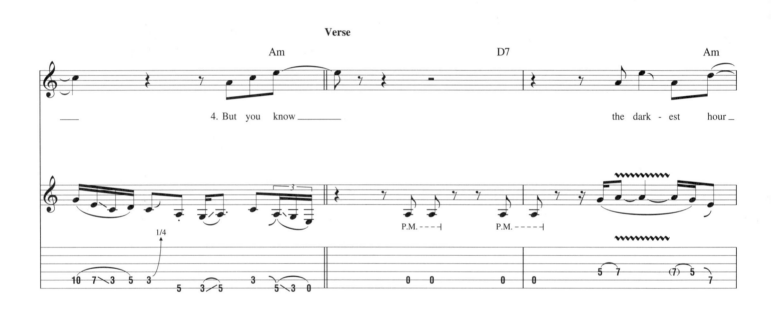

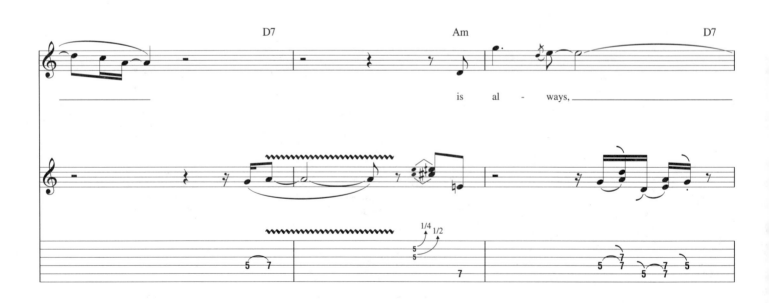

from *Carry On*

Love the One You're With

Words and Music by Stephen Stills

Open E5 tuning, down 2 steps:
(low to high) C-C↓-C-C↓-G-C

Intro
Moderately ♩ = 97

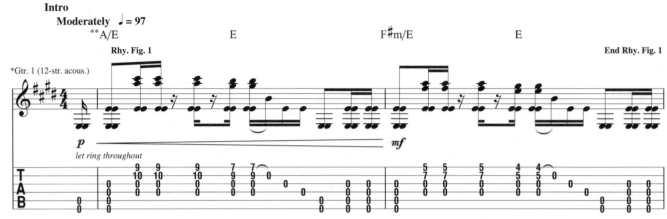

**Chord symbols reflect overall harmony (relative to detuned guitars).

*Three gtrs. arr. for one.

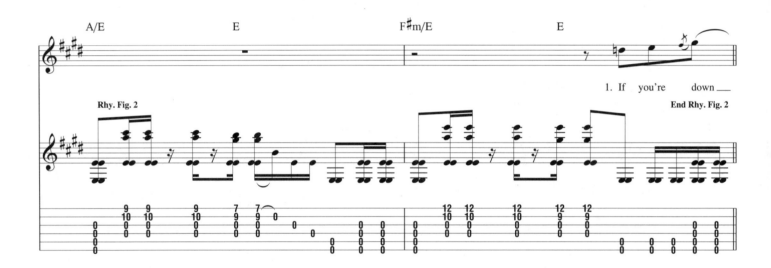

§ Verse
Gtr. 1: w/ Rhy. Fig. 1 (4 times)

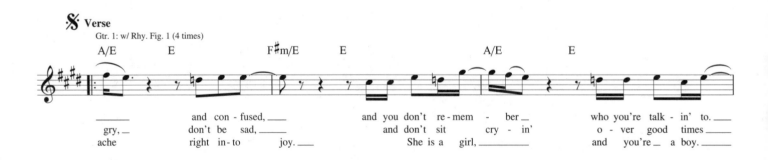

gry,— and con - fused,— and you don't re - mem - ber— who you're talk - in' to.—
don't be sad,— and don't sit cry - in' o - ver good times—
ache right in - to joy.— She is a girl,— and you're a boy.

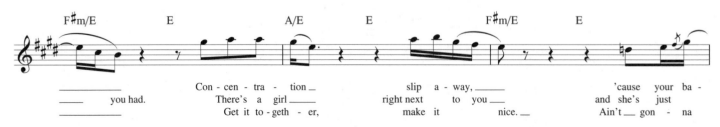

_____ you had. Con - cen - tra - tion— slip a - way,— 'cause your ba -
_____ There's a girl— right next to you— and she's just
Get it to - geth - er, make it nice.— Ain't gon - na

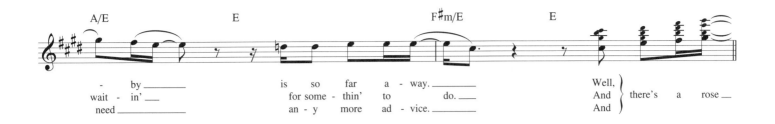

-by _____ is so far a-way. _____ Well, And there's a rose _____
wait-in' _____ for some-thin' to do. _____ And
need _____ an-y more ad-vice. _____ And

Pre-Chorus

_____ in the fist-ed glove _____ and the ea-

Gtr. 1: w/ Rhy. Fig. 3 (2 times)

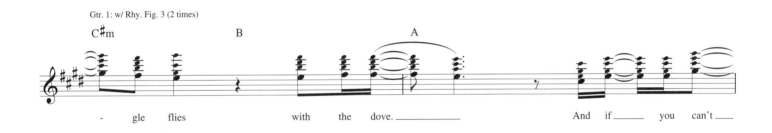

-gle flies with the dove. _____ And if _____ you can't _____

_____ be with the one _____ you love, _____ hon-ey, love the one _____ you're with.

Chorus

To Coda ⊕

Gtr. 1: w/ Rhy. Fig. 1

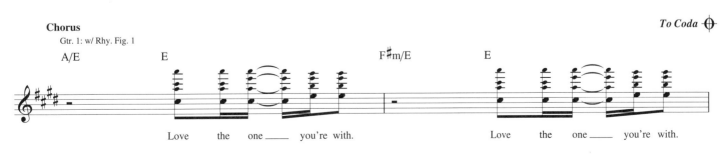

Love the one _____ you're with. Love the one _____ you're with.

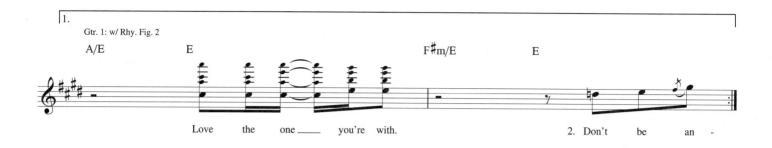

Love the one ___ you're with.   2. Don't be an -

Bridge

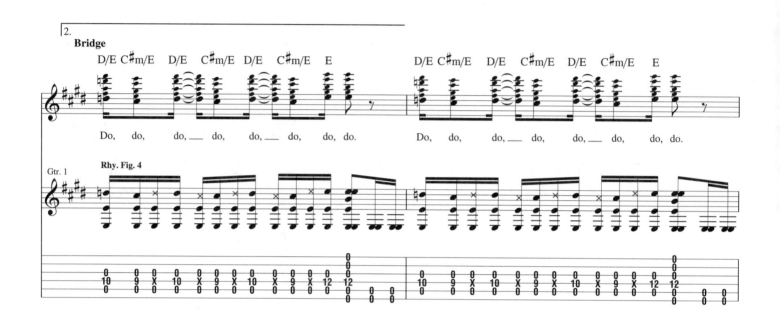

Do, do, do, ___ do, do, ___ do, do, do.   Do, do, do, ___ do, do, ___ do, do, do.

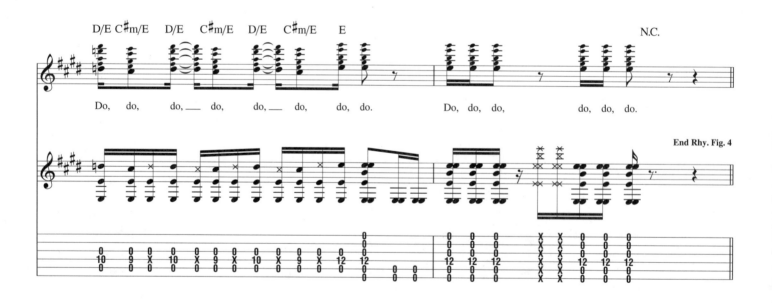

Do, do, do, ___ do, do, ___ do, do, do.   Do, do, do,   do, do, do.

Organ Solo

Gtr. 1: w/ Rhy. Fig. 3 (3 times)

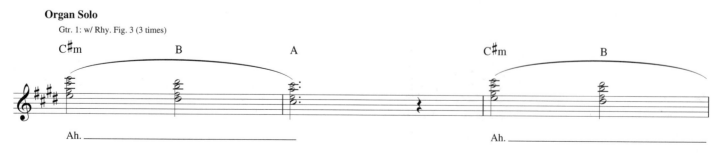

Ah. ___   Ah. ___

90

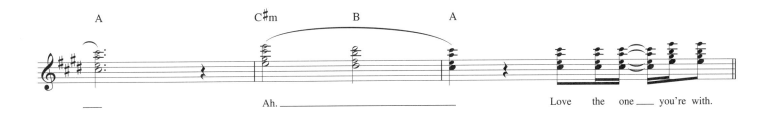

A   C#m   B   A

Ah.   Love the one ___ you're with.

Chorus

Gtr. 1: w/ Rhy. Fig. 1

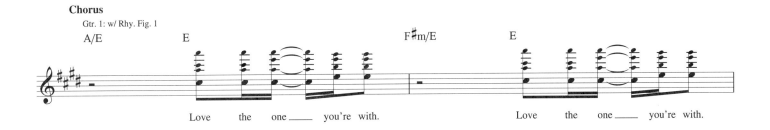

A/E   E   F#m/E   E

Love the one ___ you're with.   Love the one ___ you're with.

D.S. al Coda

Gtr. 1: w/ Rhy. Fig. 2

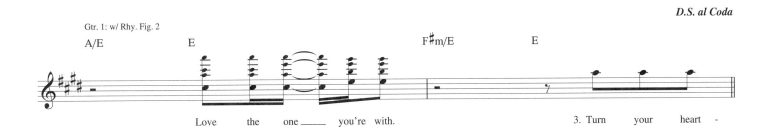

A/E   E   F#m/E   E

Love the one ___ you're with.   3. Turn your heart -

Coda

Gtr. 1: w/ Rhy. Fig. 2

A/E   E   F#m/E   E

Love the one ___ you're with.

Outro

Gtr. 1: w/ Rhy. Fig. 4

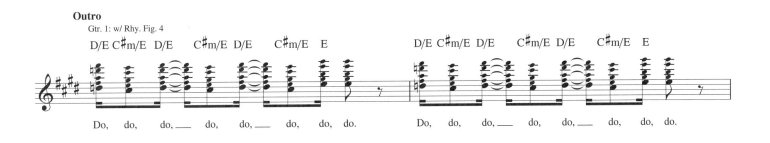

D/E C#m/E D/E   C#m/E D/E   C#m/E E   D/E C#m/E D/E   C#m/E D/E   C#m/E E

Do, do, do, ___ do, do, ___ do, do, do.   Do, do, do, ___ do, do, ___ do, do, do.

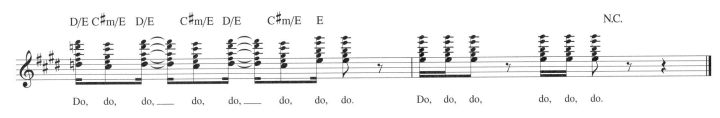

D/E C#m/E D/E   C#m/E D/E   C#m/E E   N.C.

Do, do, do, ___ do, do, ___ do, do, do.   Do, do, do,   do, do, do.

Marrakesh Express

Words and Music by Graham Nash

Verse

Gtr. 3: w/ Rhy. Fig. 1 (2 times)

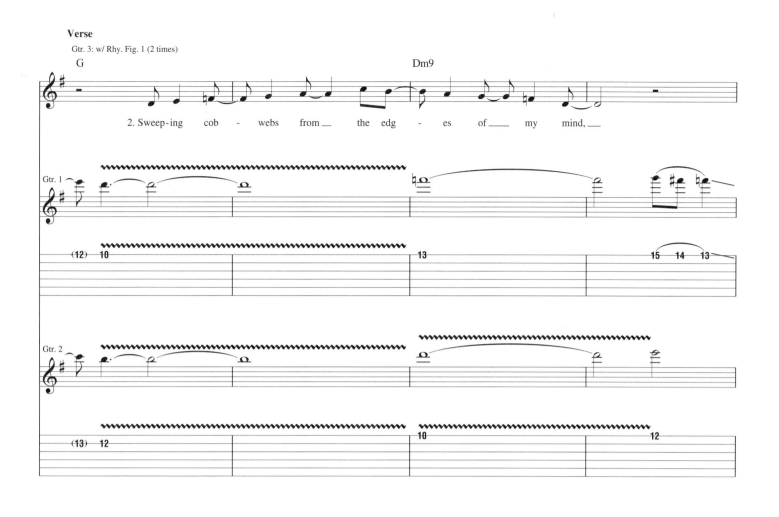

2. Sweep-ing cob - webs from __ the edg - es of __ my mind, __

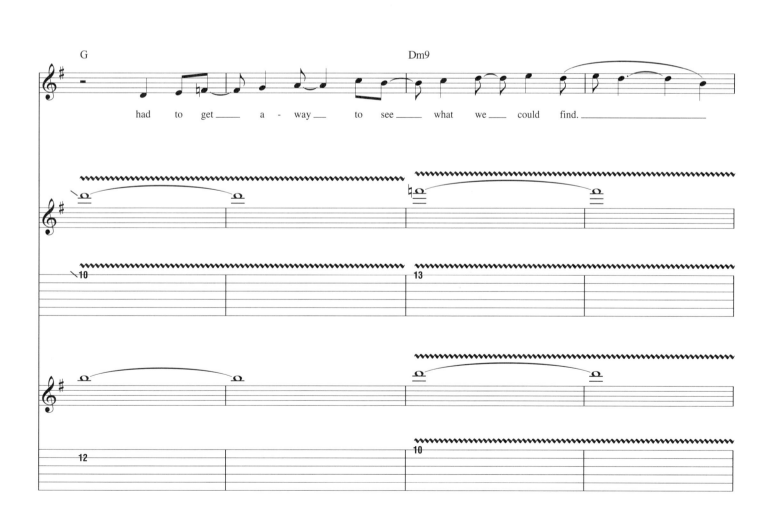

had to get __ a - way __ to see __ what we __ could find. __

Gtr. 3: w/ Rhy. Fig. 2

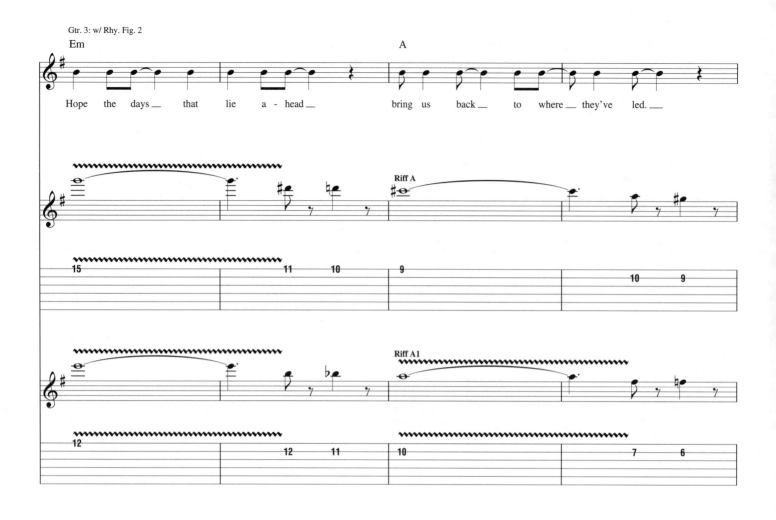

Hope the days __ that lie a - head __ bring us back __ to where __ they've led. __

Riff A

Riff A1

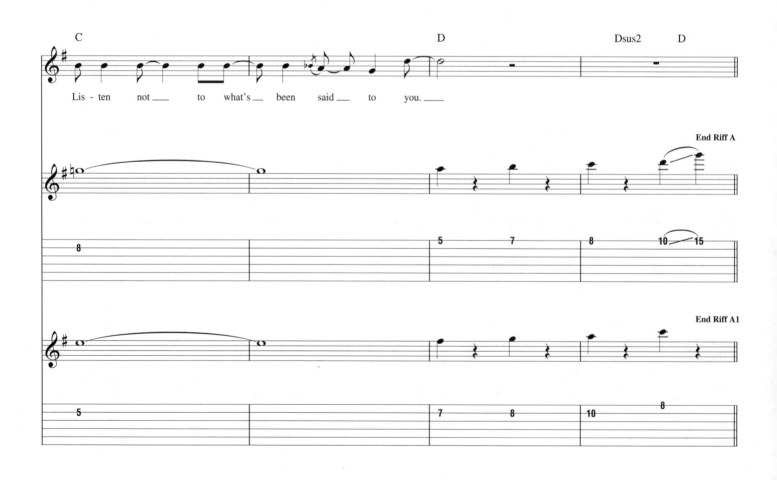

Lis - ten not __ to what's __ been said __ to you. __

End Riff A

End Riff A1

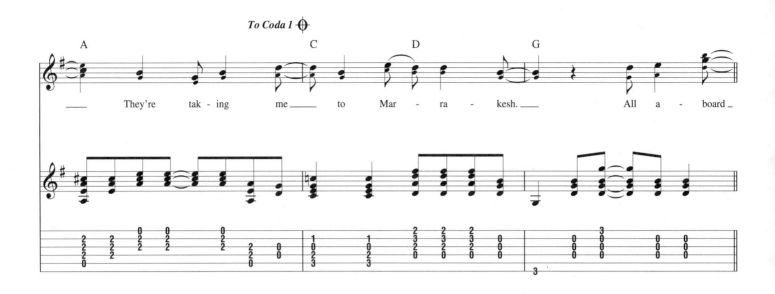

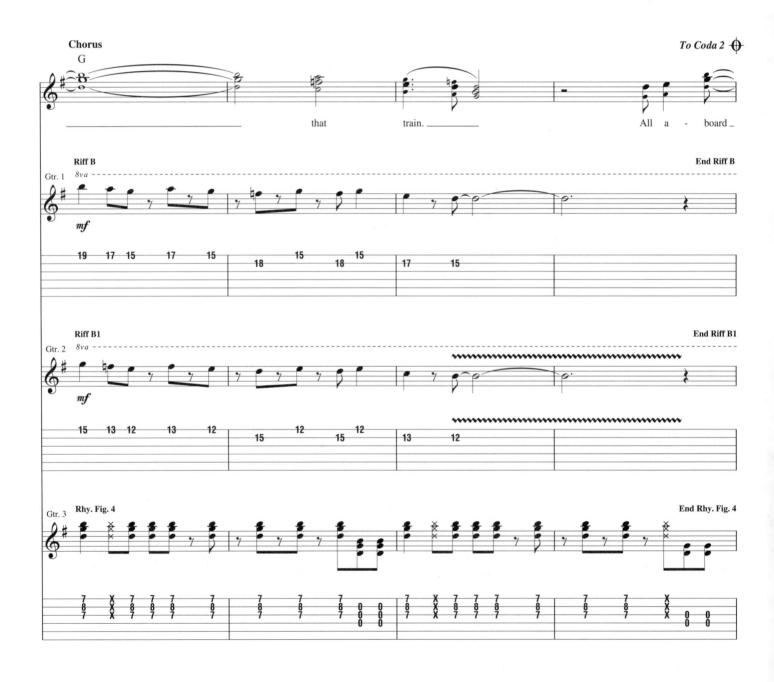

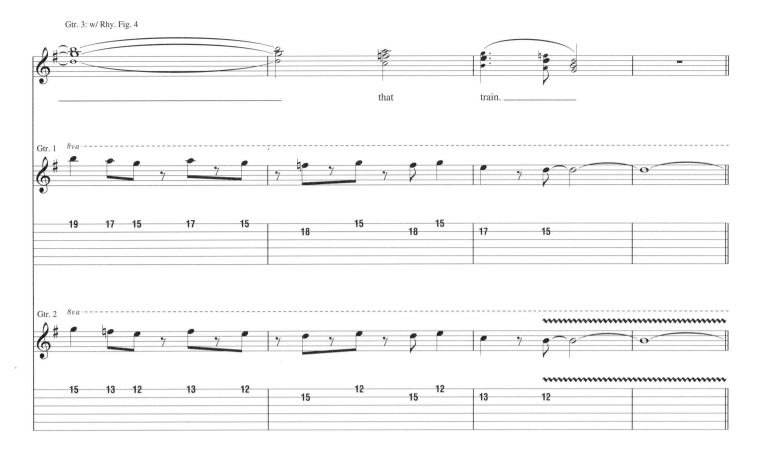

that train.

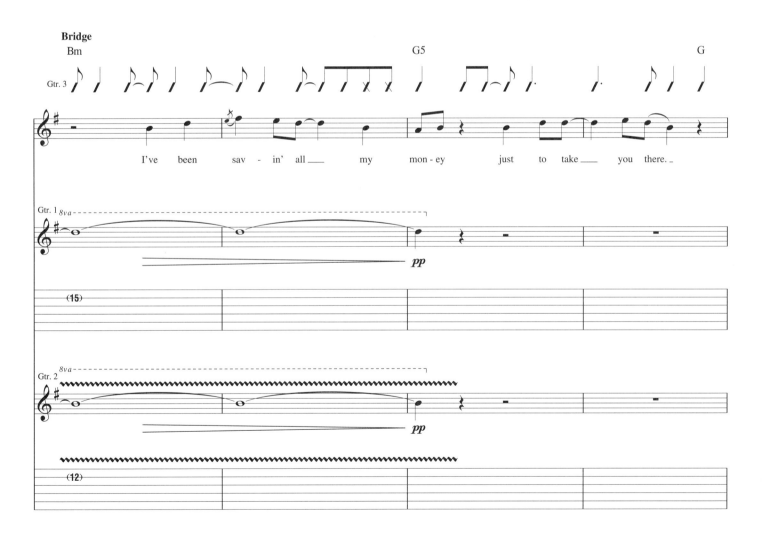

Bridge

I've been sav - in' all my mon - ey just to take you there.

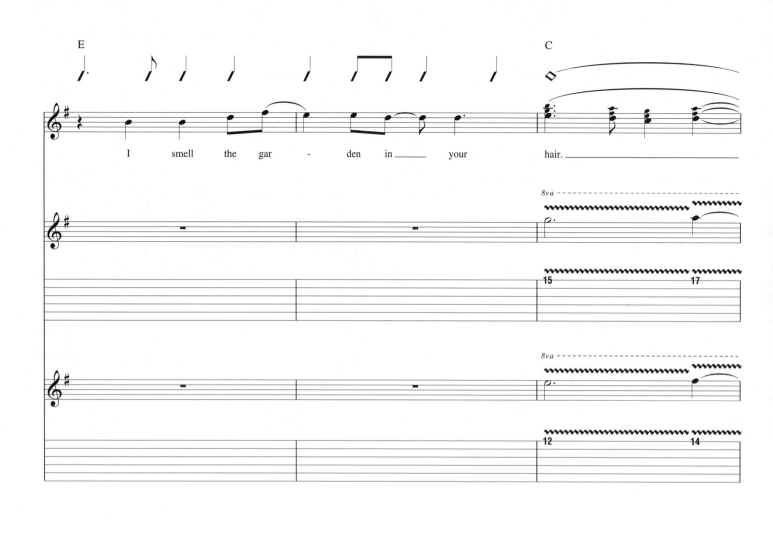

I smell the gar - den in _____ your hair. _____

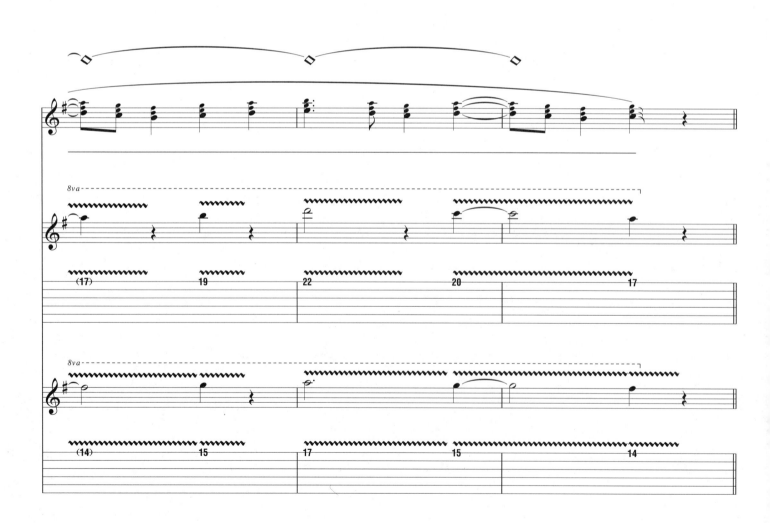

Verse

Gtr. 3: w/ Rhy. Fig. 1 (2 times)

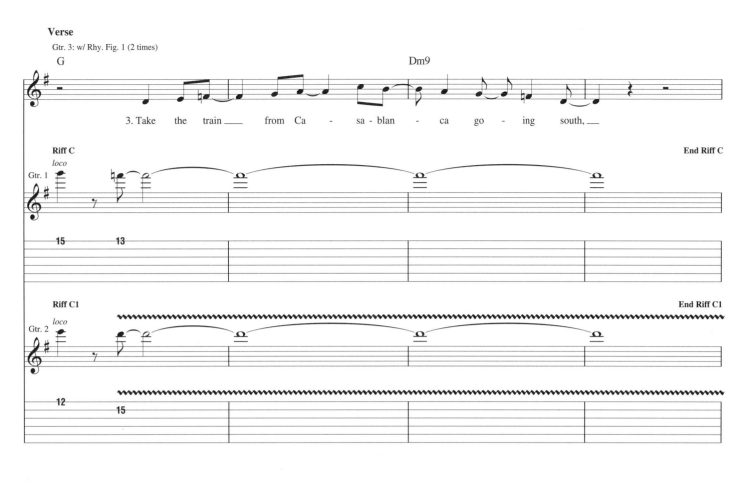

3. Take the train __ from Ca - sa - blan - ca go - ing south, __

Gtrs. 1 & 2: w/ Riffs C & C1

blow - ing smoke __ rings from the cor - ners of __ my mou - mou - mou - mou-mouth.

*Gtr. 1 notated to right of slash in tab.

striped djel - leb - as we __ can wear __ at home. Well, let me hear you, now. __

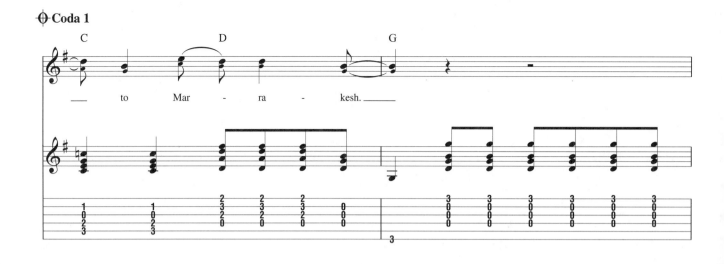

Coda 1

to Mar - ra - kesh. ____

Gtr. 3: w/ Rhy. Fig. 3

D.S.S. al Coda 2

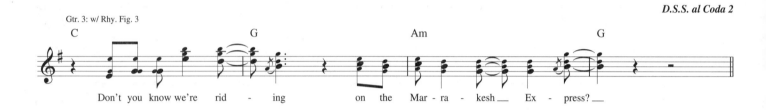

Don't you know we're rid - ing on the Mar - ra - kesh___ Ex - press? ___

Coda 2

Gtrs. 1 & 2: w/ Riffs B & B1
Gtr. 3: w/ Rhy. Fig. 4

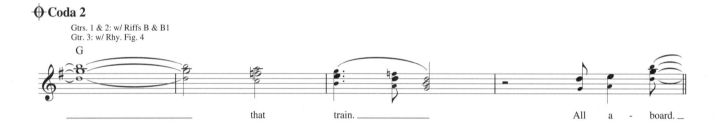

_____ that train. _____ All a - board. ___

Outro

Gtrs. 1 & 2: w/ Riffs B & B1 (last 2 meas., till fade)

Dm9/G

Gtr. 3

Rhy. Fig. 5   End Rhy. Fig. 5

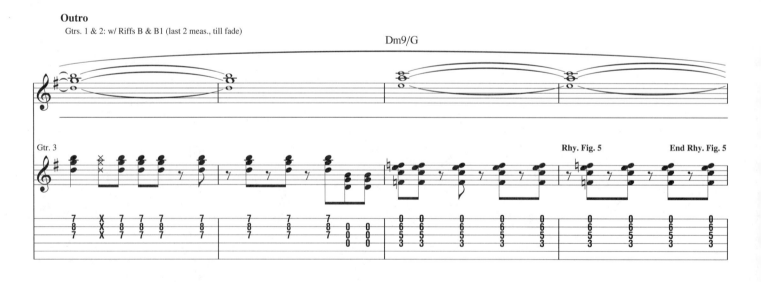

Gtr. 3: w/ Rhy. Fig. 5 (till fade)

Begin fade   *Fade out*

from *Déjà Vu*
Our House
Words and Music by Graham Nash

from *CSN*
Shadow Captain
Words and Music by David Crosby and Craig Doerge

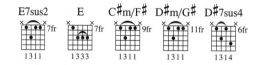

*Piano arr. for gtr.

1. Oh, Cap -

*Chord symbols reflect implied harmony.

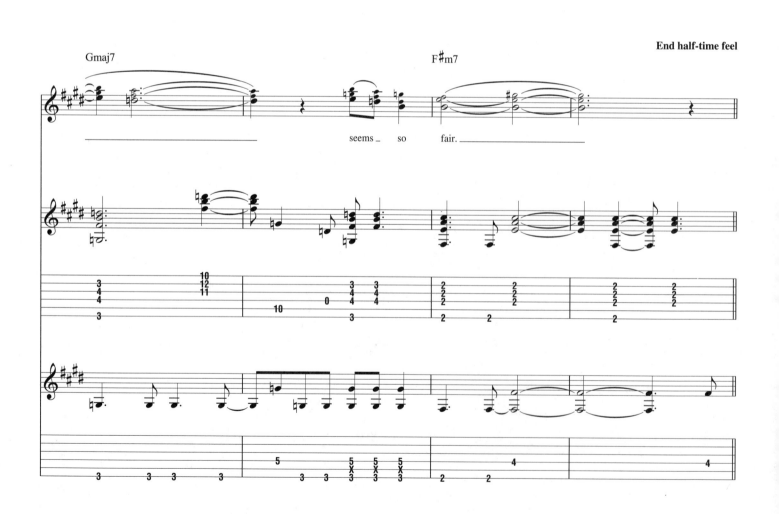

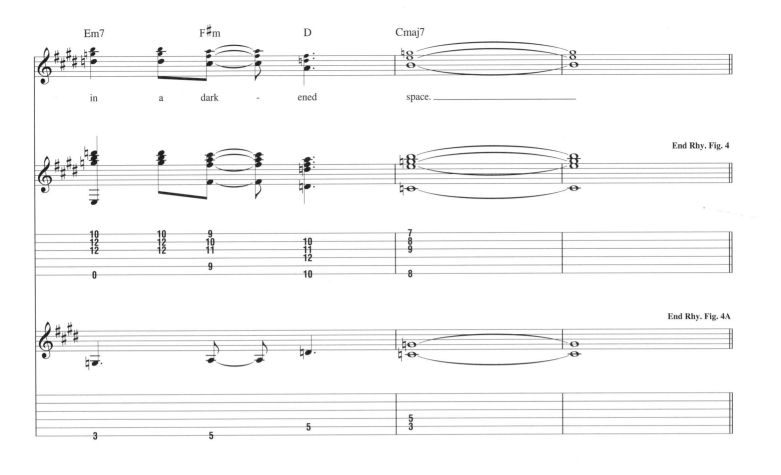

in a dark - ened space. _____

End Rhy. Fig. 4

End Rhy. Fig. 4A

Interlude

Gtr. 2: w/ Rhy. Fig. 1A (1 1/2 times)

Gtr. 1: w/ Rhy. Fig. 2

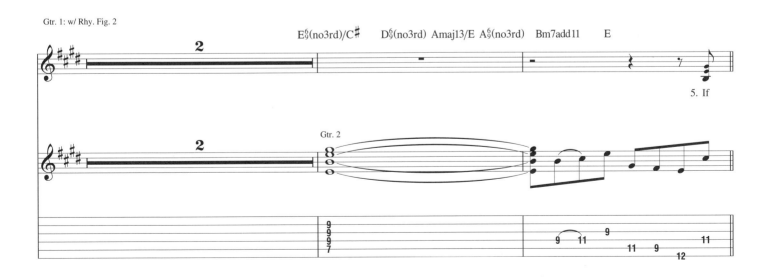

5. If

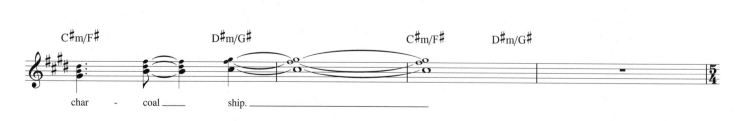

Try - ing to give ___ the light the slip. ___

*Unison vocals

Outro
Gtrs. 1 & 2: w/ Rhy. Figs. 1 & 1A (1 1/2 times)

*Vol. swell

117

from *Carry On*

Southern Cross

Words and Music by Stephen Stills, Richard Curtis and Michael Curtis

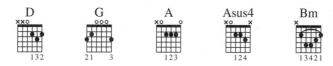

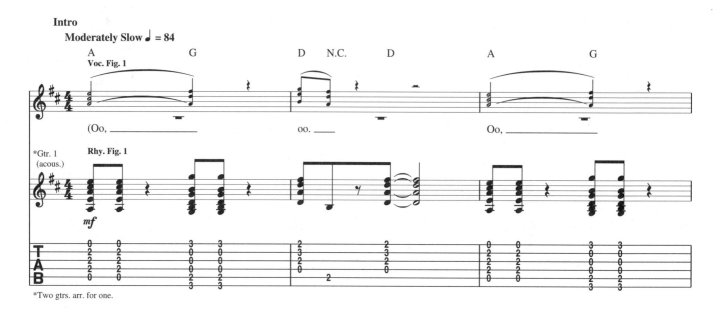

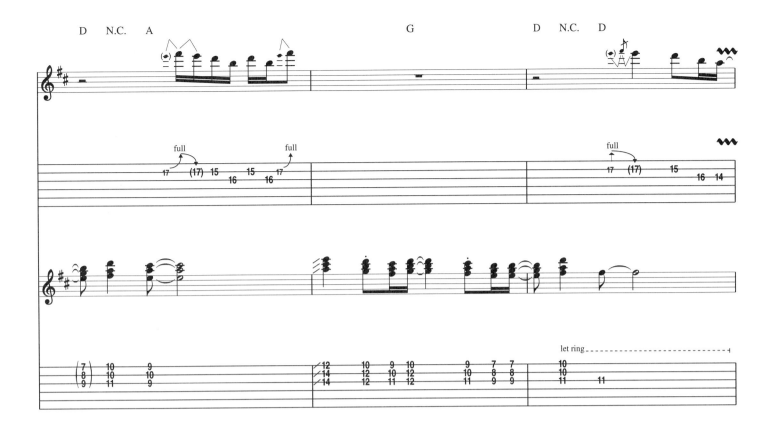

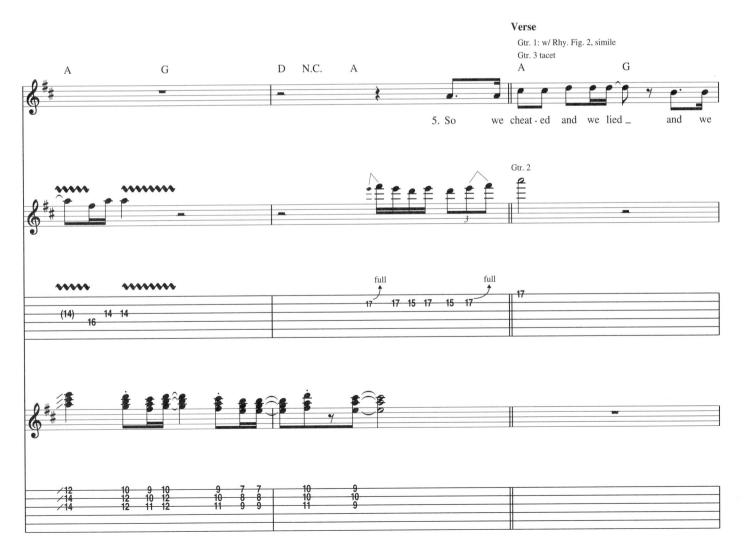

5. So we cheat-ed and we lied _ and we

Verse
Gtr. 1: w/ Rhy. Fig. 2, simile
Gtr. 3 tacet

test - ed.   And we nev - er failed to fail;   it was the eas - i - est thing to do. __

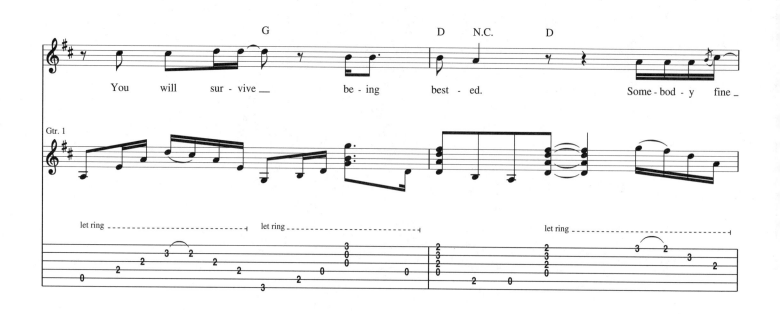

You   will   sur - vive __   be - ing   best - ed.   Some - bod - y fine __

__   will come a - long, make me for - get a - bout lov - ing   you   at the South - ern

Cross.

from *Crosby, Stills & Nash*

Suite: Judy Blue Eyes

Words and Music by Stephen Stills

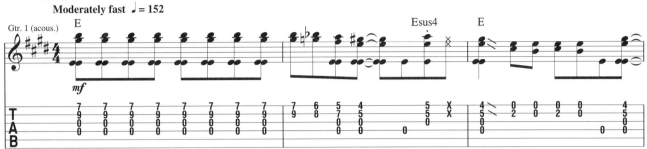

Gtrs. 1, 2 & 4: Open E5 tuning:
(low to high) E-B-E-E-B-E

Intro

Moderately fast ♩ = 152

1. It's

(cont. in slashes)

Verse

1st time, Gtr. 2 tacet
2nd time, Gtrs. 1, 2 & 3: w/ Rhy. Fills 2 & 2A

get - ting   to   the   point ____   where   I'm   no   and
mem - ber   what ___ we've   said ____   and   done   and

* Composite arrangement
**T = Thumb on 6th string

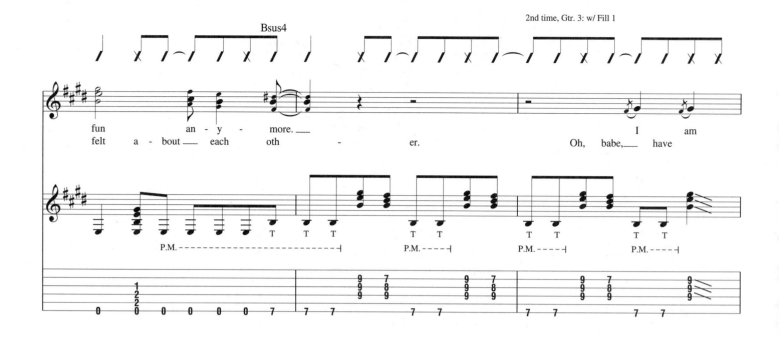

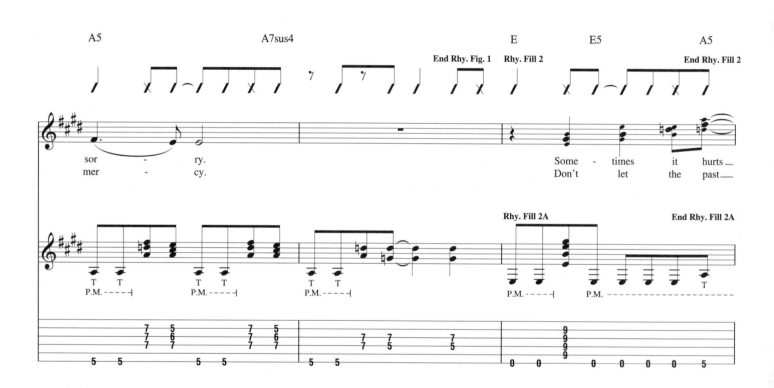

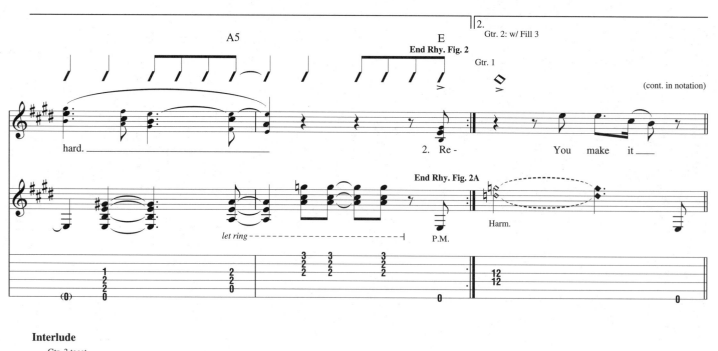

Interlude

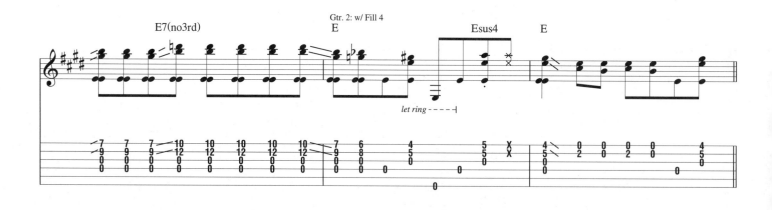

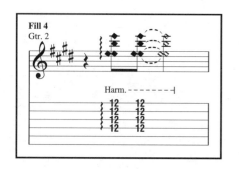

Bridge

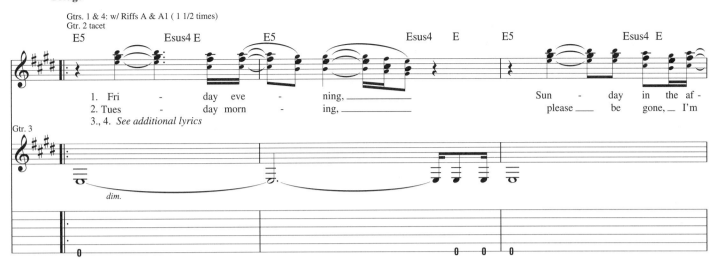

Gtrs. 1 & 4: w/ Riffs A & A1 (1 1/2 times)
Gtr. 2 tacet

1. Fri - day eve - ning, _____
2. Tues - day morn - ing, _____
3., 4. *See additional lyrics*

Sun - day in the af -
please _____ be gone, _____ I'm

Gtr. 3

dim.

1.,3.

3rd & 4th times, Gtr. 3: w/ Fill 5

1st, 2nd & 3rd times, Gtr. 1: w/ Riff A
4th time, Gtr. 1: w/ Riff A (1st meas.)
Gtr. 4: w/ Riff A1

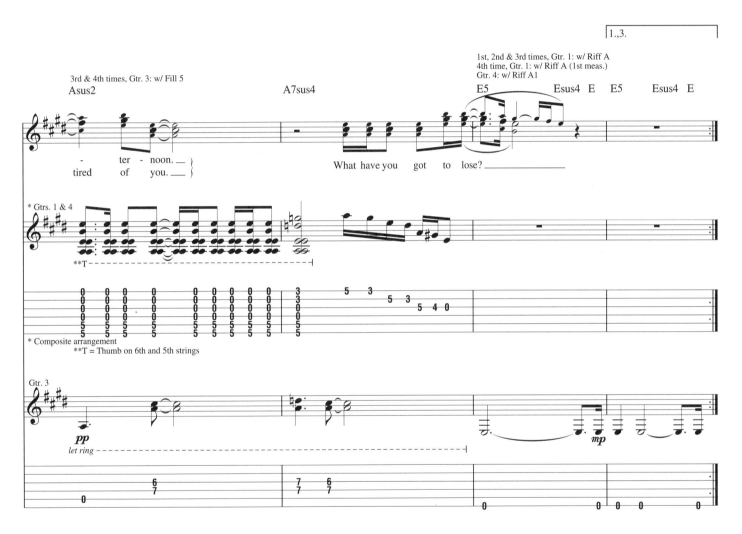

- ter - noon. }
tired of you. _____ }

What have you got to lose? _____

* Gtrs. 1 & 4

T- -

* Composite arrangement
**T = Thumb on 6th and 5th strings

Gtr. 3

pp
let ring - |

mp

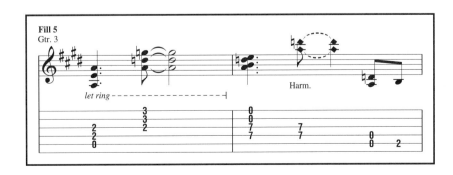

Fill 5
Gtr. 3

let ring - - - - - - - - - - - - - - |

Harm.

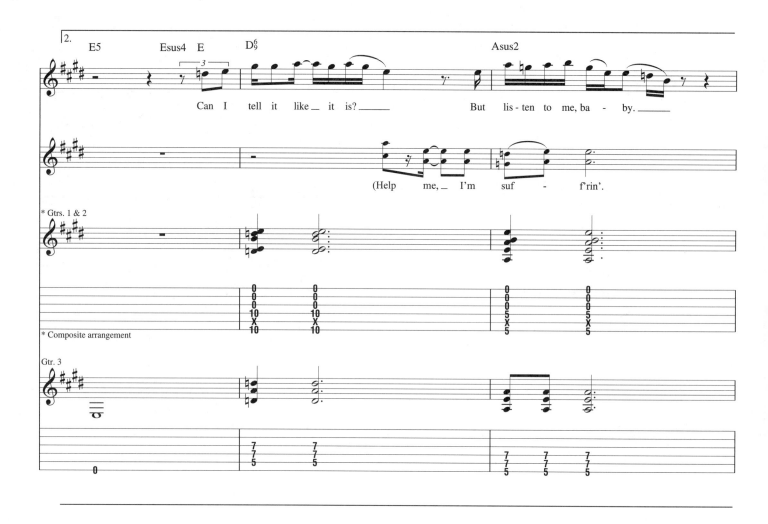

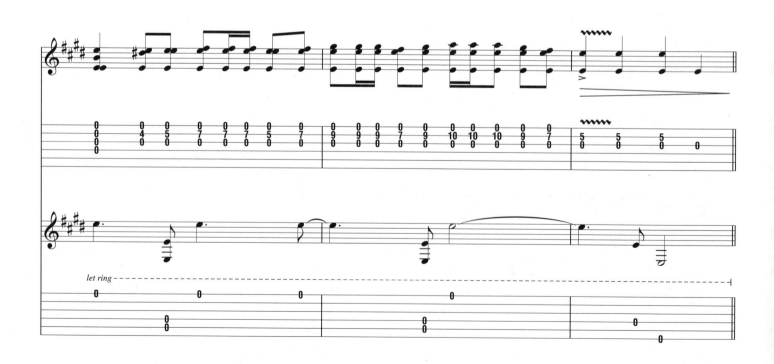

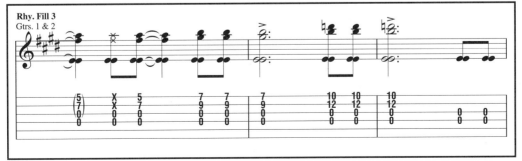

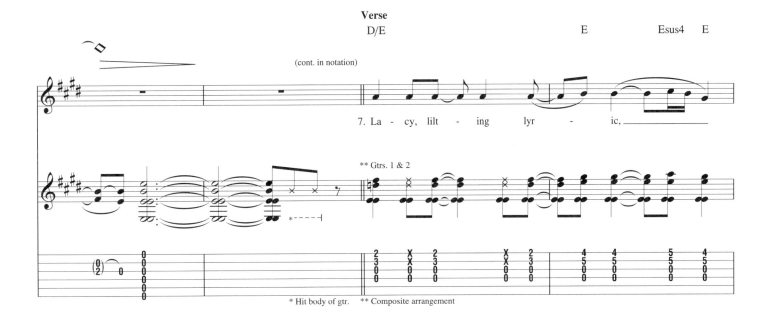

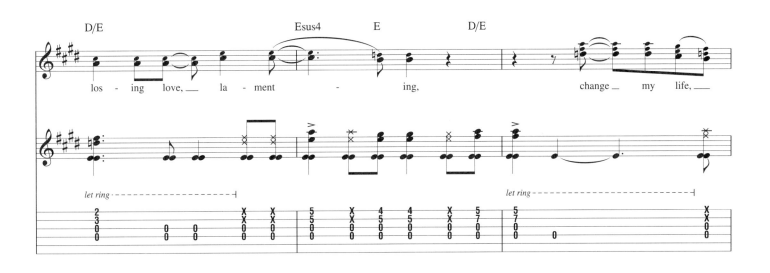

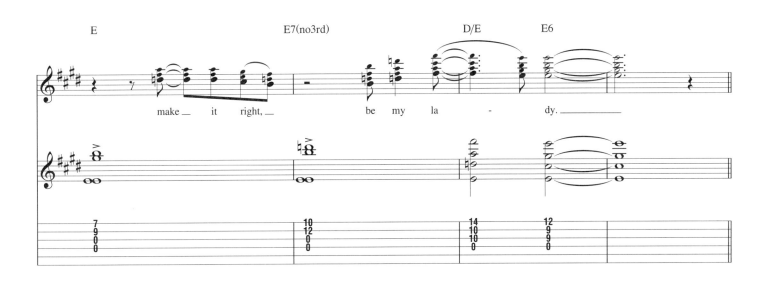

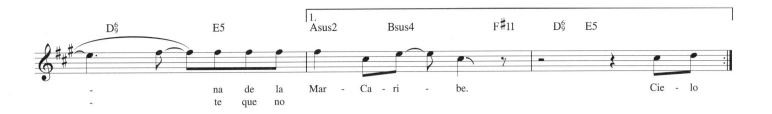

na de la Mar Ca - ri - be.   Cie - lo
te que no

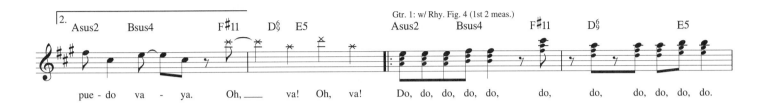

pue - do va - ya.   Oh,___ va! Oh, va!   Do, do, do, do, do,   do,   do,   do, do, do, do.

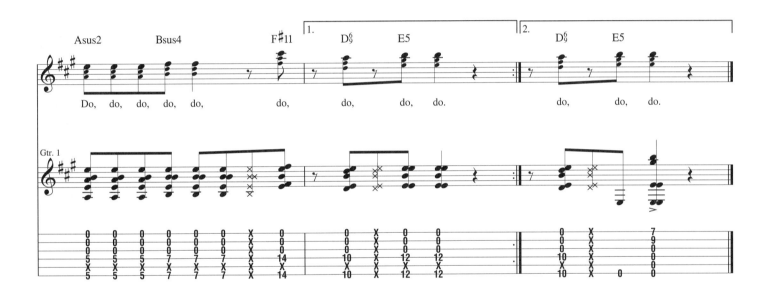

Do, do, do, do, do,   do,   do,   do,   do.   do,   do,   do.

Additional Lyrics

Bridge:
3. I've got an answer,
   I'm going to fly away.
   What have I got to lose?

4. Will you come see me
   Thursdays and Saturdays? Hey, (hey,) hey.
   What have you got to lose?

Outro translation:
How happy it makes me to think of Cuba,
The smiles of the Caribbean Sea.
Sunny sky has no blood,
And how sad that I'm not able to go.
Oh, go! Oh, go!

from *Déjà Vu*

Teach Your Children

Words and Music by Graham Nash

143

* vol. swells

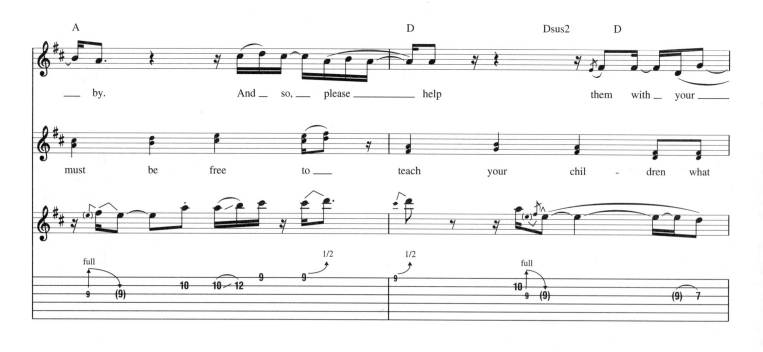

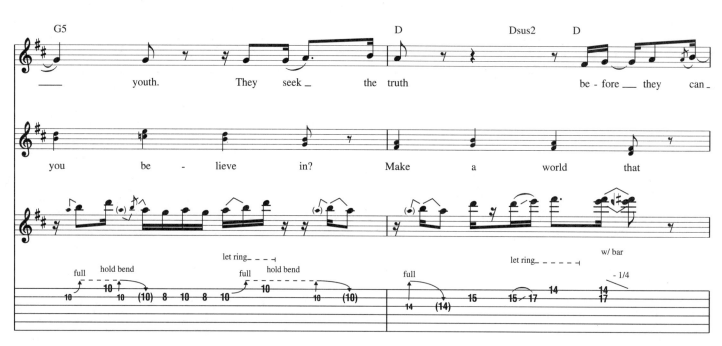

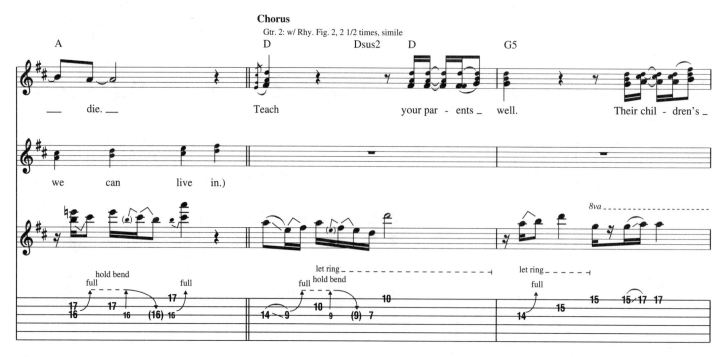

146

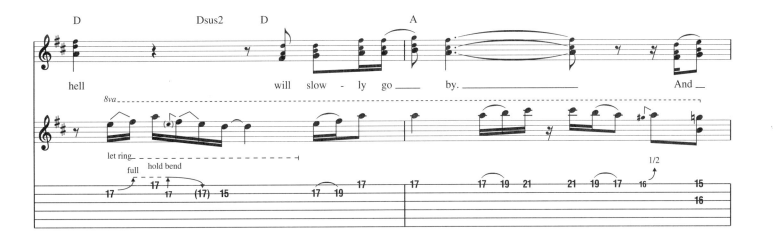

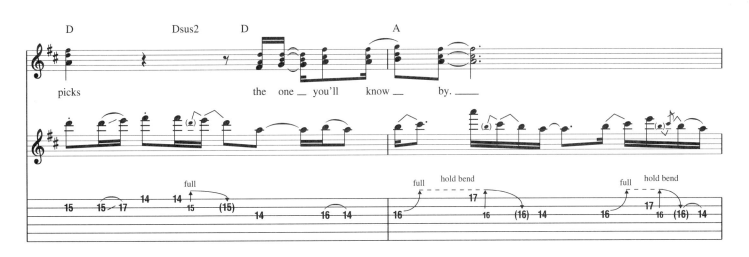

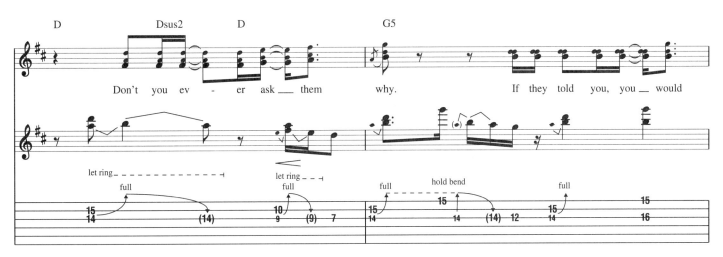

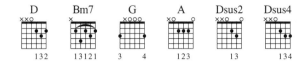

from *Daylight Again*
Wasted on the Way
Words and Music by Graham Nash

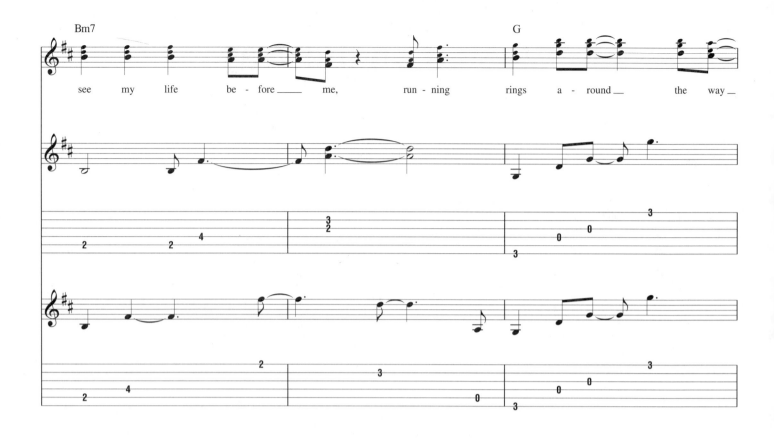

see my life be-fore _____ me, run-ning rings a-round _____ the way _____

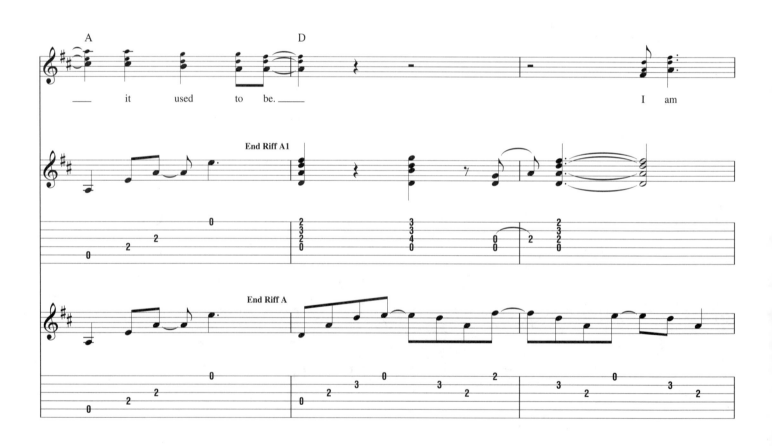

_____ it used to be. _____ I am

End Riff A1

End Riff A

Gtrs. 1 & 3: w/ Riffs A & A1

old - er now, I have more than what I want -

-ed, but I wish that I _____ had start - ed long be - fore ___

_____ I did. And there's

Gtr. 3

Gtr. 1

🎵 Chorus

so much time } to make up ev - 'ry - where ___ you turn, ___
So much love }

Riff B
*Gtrs. 1, 2 & 3

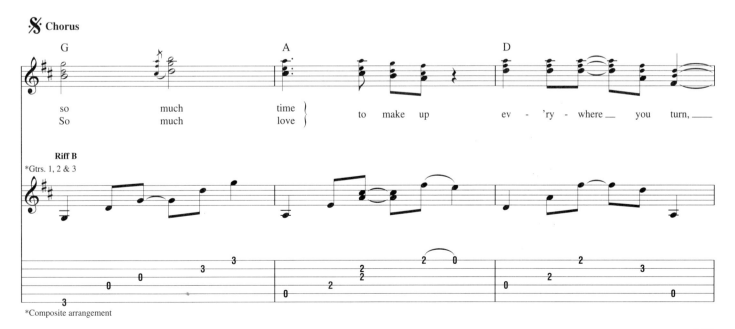

*Composite arrangement

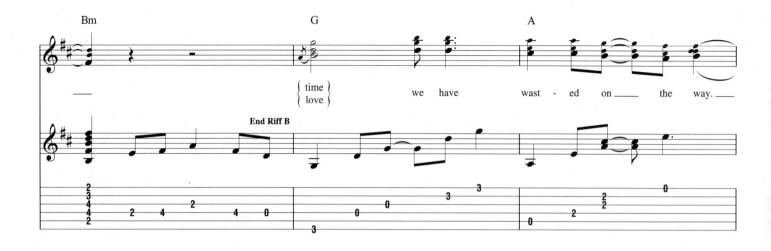

we have wast-ed on ___ the way. ___

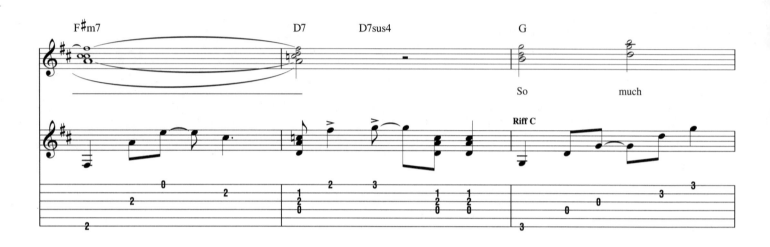

So much

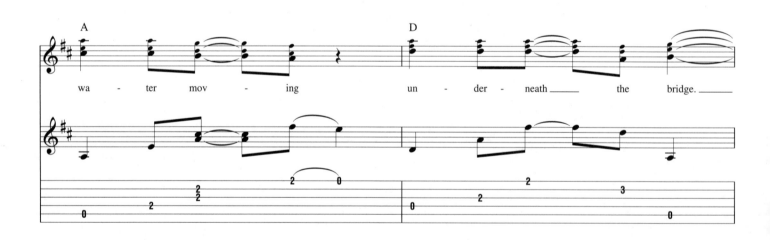

wa - ter mov - ing un - der - neath ___ the bridge. ___

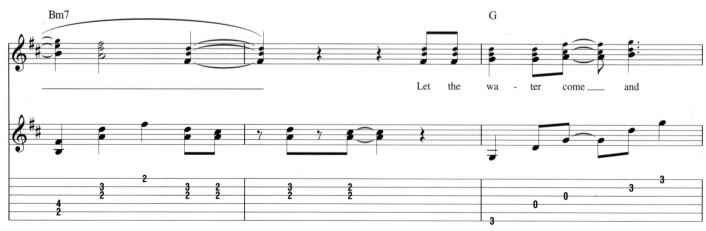

Let the wa - ter come ___ and

153

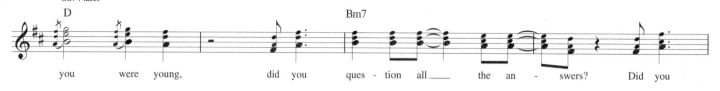

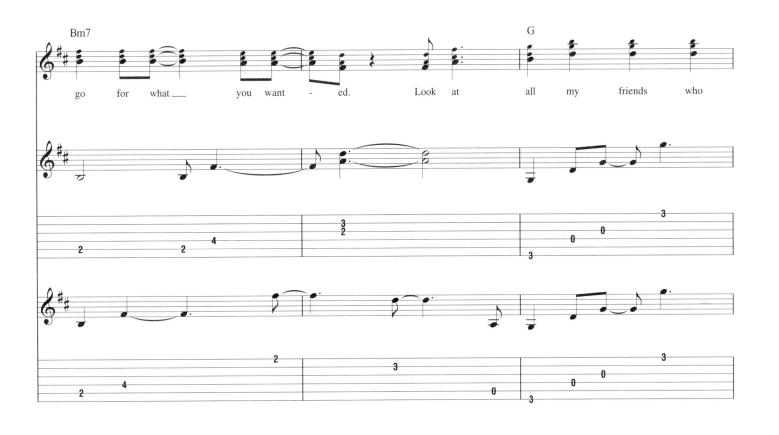

Chorus

Gtrs. 1, 2 & 3: w/ Riff B

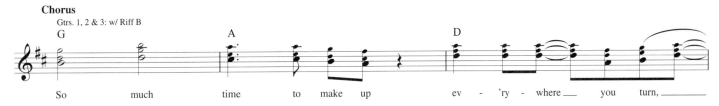

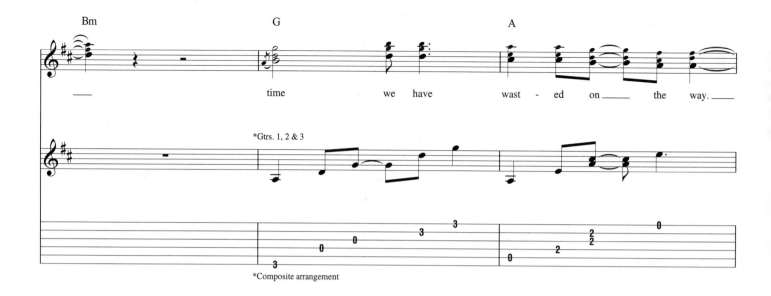

time we have wast - ed on ____ the way. ____

*Gtrs. 1, 2 & 3

*Composite arrangement

Gtrs. 1, 2 & 3: w/ Riff C

So much

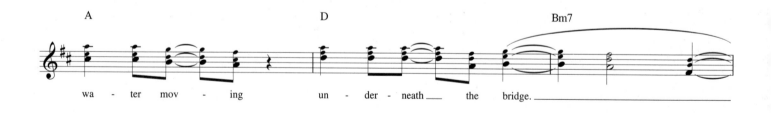

wa - ter mov - ing un - der - neath ____ the bridge. ____

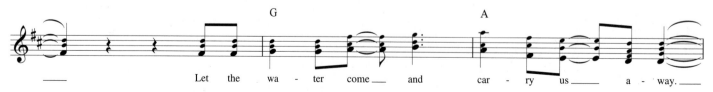

Let the wa - ter come ____ and car - ry us ____ a - way. ____

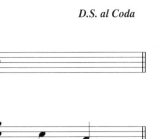

D.S. al Coda

*Gtrs. 1, 2 & 3

*Composite arrangement.

Coda

Let the wa - ter come ____ and

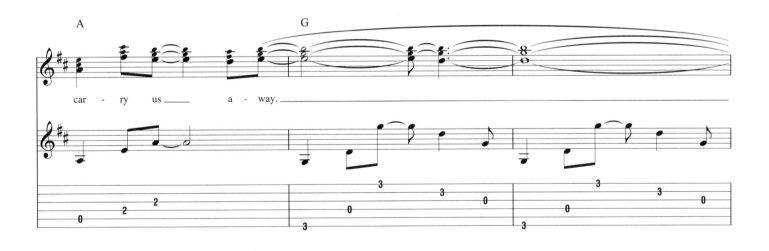

car - ry us ____ a - way. ____

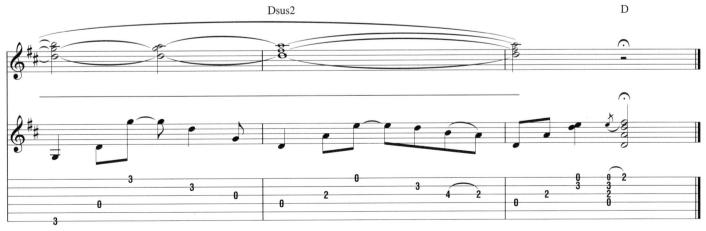

157

Guitar Notation Legend

Guitar Music can be notated three different ways: on a *musical staff*, in *tablature*, and in *rhythm slashes*.

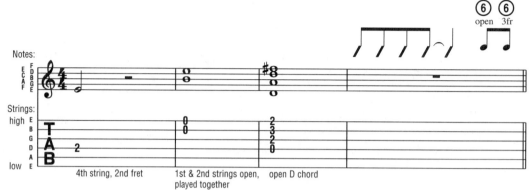

RHYTHM SLASHES are written above the staff. Strum chords in the rhythm indicated. Use the chord diagrams found at the top of the first page of the transcription for the appropriate chord voicings. Round noteheads indicate single notes.

THE MUSICAL STAFF shows pitches and rhythms and is divided by bar lines into measures. Pitches are named after the first seven letters of the alphabet.

TABLATURE graphically represents the guitar fingerboard. Each horizontal line represents a string, and each number represents a fret.

4th string, 2nd fret　　1st & 2nd strings open, played together　　open D chord

HALF-STEP BEND: Strike the note and bend up 1/2 step.

WHOLE-STEP BEND: Strike the note and bend up one step.

GRACE NOTE BEND: Strike the note and immediately bend up as indicated.

SLIGHT (MICROTONE) BEND: Strike the note and bend up 1/4 step.

BEND AND RELEASE: Strike the note and bend up as indicated, then release back to the original note. Only the first note is struck.

PRE-BEND: Bend the note as indicated, then strike it.

VIBRATO: The string is vibrated by rapidly bending and releasing the note with the fretting hand.

WIDE VIBRATO: The pitch is varied to a greater degree by vibrating with the fretting hand.

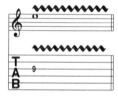

HAMMER-ON: Strike the first (lower) note with one finger, then sound the higher note (on the same string) with another finger by fretting it without picking.

PULL-OFF: Place both fingers on the notes to be sounded. Strike the first note and without picking, pull the finger off to sound the second (lower) note.

LEGATO SLIDE: Strike the first note and then slide the same fret-hand finger up or down to the second note. The second note is not struck.

SHIFT SLIDE: Same as legato slide, except the second note is struck.

TRILL: Very rapidly alternate between the notes indicated by continuously hammering on and pulling off.

TAPPING: Hammer ("tap") the fret indicated with the pick-hand index or middle finger and pull off to the note fretted by the fret hand.

NATURAL HARMONIC: Strike the note while the fret-hand lightly touches the string directly over the fret indicated.

PINCH HARMONIC: The note is fretted normally and a harmonic is produced by adding the edge of the thumb or the tip of the index finger of the pick hand to the normal pick attack.

PICK SCRAPE: The edge of the pick is rubbed down (or up) the string, producing a scratchy sound.

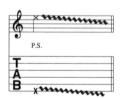

MUFFLED STRINGS: A percussive sound is produced by laying the fret hand across the string(s) without depressing, and striking them with the pick hand.

PALM MUTING: The note is partially muted by the pick hand lightly touching the string(s) just before the bridge.

RAKE: Drag the pick across the strings indicated with a single motion.

TREMOLO PICKING: The note is picked as rapidly and continuously as possible.

VIBRATO BAR DIVE AND RETURN: The pitch of the note or chord is dropped a specified number of steps (in rhythm) then returned to the original pitch.

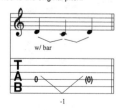

VIBRATO BAR SCOOP: Depress the bar just before striking the note, then quickly release the bar.

VIBRATO BAR DIP: Strike the note and then immediately drop a specified number of steps, then release back to the original pitch.

RECORDED VERSIONS
The Best Note-For-Note Transcriptions Available

ALL BOOKS INCLUDE TABLATURE

HAL•LEONARD® GUITAR PLAY•ALONG

This series will help you play your favorite songs quickly and easily. Just follow the tab and listen to the CD to hear how the guitar should sound, and then play along using the separate backing tracks. Mac or PC users can also slow down the tempo by using the CD in their computer. The melody and lyrics are included in the book so that you can sing or simply follow along.

INCLUDES TAB

VOL. 1 – ROCK GUITAR 00699570 / $12.95
Day Tripper • Message in a Bottle • Refugee • Shattered • Sunshine of Your Love • Takin' Care of Business • Tush • Walk This Way.

VOL. 2 – ACOUSTIC 00699569 / $12.95
Angie • Behind Blue Eyes • Best of My Love • Blackbird • Dust in the Wind • Layla • Night Moves • Yesterday.

VOL. 3 – HARD ROCK 00699573 / $14.95
Crazy Train • Iron Man • Living After Midnight • Rock You Like a Hurricane • Round and Round • Smoke on the Water • Sweet Child O' Mine • You Really Got Me.

VOL. 4 – POP/ROCK 00699571 / $12.95
Breakdown • Crazy Little Thing Called Love • Hit Me with Your Best Shot • I Want You to Want Me • Lights • R.O.C.K. in the U.S.A. • Summer of '69 • What I Like About You.

VOL. 5 – MODERN ROCK 00699574 / $12.95
Aerials • Alive • Bother • Chop Suey! • Control • Last Resort • Take a Look Around (Theme from *M:I-2*) • Wish You Were Here.

VOL. 6 – '90S ROCK 00699572 / $12.95
Are You Gonna Go My Way • Come Out and Play • I'll Stick Around • Know Your Enemy • Man in the Box • Outshined • Smells Like Teen Spirit • Under the Bridge.

VOL. 7 – BLUES GUITAR 00699575 / $12.95
All Your Love (I Miss Loving) • Born Under a Bad Sign • Hide Away • I'm Tore Down • I'm Your Hoochie Coochie Man • Pride and Joy • Sweet Home Chicago • The Thrill Is Gone.

VOL. 8 – ROCK 00699585 / $12.95
All Right Now • Black Magic Woman • Get Back • Hey Joe • Layla • Love Me Two Times • Won't Get Fooled Again • You Really Got Me.

VOL. 9 – PUNK ROCK 00699576 / $12.95
All the Small Things • Fat Lip • Flavor of the Weak • I Feel So • Lifestyles of the Rich and Famous• Say It Ain't So • Self Esteem • (So) Tired of Waiting for You.

VOL. 10 – ACOUSTIC 00699586 / $12.95
Here Comes the Sun • Landslide • The Magic Bus • Norwegian Wood (This Bird Has Flown) • Pink Houses • Space Oddity • Tangled Up in Blue • Tears in Heaven.

VOL. 11 – EARLY ROCK 00699579 / $12.95
Fun, Fun, Fun • Hound Dog • Louie, Louie • No Particular Place to Go • Oh, Pretty Woman • Rock Around the Clock • Under the Boardwalk • Wild Thing.

VOL. 12 – POP/ROCK 00699587 / $12.95
867-5309/Jenny • Every Breath You Take • Money for Nothing • Rebel, Rebel • Run to You • Ticket to Ride • Wonderful Tonight • You Give Love a Bad Name.

VOL. 13 – FOLK ROCK 00699581 / $12.95
Annie's Song • Leaving on a Jet Plane • Suite: Judy Blue Eyes • This Land Is Your Land • Time in a Bottle • Turn! Turn! Turn! • You've Got a Friend • You've Got to Hide Your Love Away.

VOL. 14 – BLUES ROCK 00699582 / $14.95
Blue on Black • Crossfire • Cross Road Blues (Crossroads) • The House Is Rockin' • La Grange • Move It on Over • Roadhouse Blues • Statesboro Blues.

VOL. 15 – R&B 00699583 / $12.95
Ain't Too Proud to Beg • Brick House • Get Ready • I Can't Help Myself • I Got You (I Feel Good) • I Heard It Through the Grapevine • My Girl • Shining Star.

VOL. 16 – JAZZ 00699584 / $12.95
All Blues • Bluesette • Footprints • How Insensitive • Misty • Satin Doll • Stella by Starlight • Tenor Madness.

VOL. 17 – COUNTRY 00699588 / $12.95
Amie • Boot Scootin' Boogie • Chattahoochee • Folsom Prison Blues • Friends in Low Places • Forever and Ever, Amen • T-R-O-U-B-L-E • Workin' Man Blues.

VOL. 18 – ACOUSTIC ROCK 00699577 / $14.95
About a Girl • Breaking the Girl • Drive • Iris • More Than Words • Patience • Silent Lucidity • 3 AM.

VOL. 19 – SOUL 00699578 / $12.95
Get Up (I Feel Like Being) a Sex Machine • Green Onions • In the Midnight Hour • Knock on Wood • Mustang Sally • Respect • (Sittin' On) The Dock of the Bay • Soul Man.

VOL. 20 – ROCKABILLY 00699580 / $12.95
Be-Bop-A-Lula • Blue Suede Shoes • Hello Mary Lou • Little Sister • Mystery Train • Rock This Town • Stray Cat Strut • That'll Be the Day.

VOL. 21 – YULETIDE 00699602 / $12.95
Angels We Have Heard on High • Away in a Manger • Deck the Hall • The First Noel • Go, Tell It on the Mountain • Jingle Bells • Joy to the World • O Little Town of Bethlehem.

VOL. 22 – CHRISTMAS 00699600 / $12.95
The Christmas Song (Chestnuts Roasting on an Open Fire) • Frosty the Snow Man • Happy Xmas (War Is Over) • Here Comes Santa Claus • Jingle-Bell Rock • Merry Christmas, Darling • Rudolph the Red-Nosed Reindeer • Silver Bells.

VOL. 23 – SURF 00699635 / $12.95
Let's Go Trippin' • Out of Limits • Penetration • Pipeline • Surf City • Surfin' U.S.A. • Walk Don't Run • The Wedge.

VOL. 24 – ERIC CLAPTON 00699649 / $14.95
Badge • Bell Bottom Blues • Change the World • Cocaine • Key to the Highway • Lay Down Sally • White Room • Wonderful Tonight.

VOL. 25 – LENNON & McCARTNEY 00699642 / $14.95
Back in the U.S.S.R. • Drive My Car • Get Back • A Hard Day's Night • I Feel Fine • Paperback Writer • Revolution • Ticket to Ride.

VOL. 26 – ELVIS PRESLEY 00699643 / $14.95
All Shook Up • Blue Suede Shoes • Don't Be Cruel • Heartbreak Hotel • Hound Dog • Jailhouse Rock • Little Sister • Mystery Train.

VOL. 27 – DAVID LEE ROTH 00699645 / $14.95
Ain't Talkin' 'Bout Love • Dance the Night Away • Just Like Paradise • A Lil' Ain't Enough • Panama • Runnin' with the Devil • Unchained • Yankee Rose.

VOL. 28 – GREG KOCH 00699646 / $14.95
Chief's Blues • Death of a Bassman • Dylan the Villain • The Grip • Holy Grail • Spank It • Tonus Diabolicus • Zoiks.

VOL. 29 – BOB SEGER 00699647 / $14.95
Against the Wind • Betty Lou's Gettin' Out Tonight • Hollywood Nights • Mainstreet • Night Moves • Old Time Rock & Roll • Rock and Roll Never Forgets • Still the Same.

VOL. 30 – KISS 00699644 / $14.95
Cold Gin • Detroit Rock City • Deuce • Firehouse • Heaven's on Fire • Love Gun • Rock and Roll All Nite • Shock Me.

VOL. 31 – CHRISTMAS HITS 00699652 / $12.95
Blue Christmas • Do You Hear What I Hear • Happy Holiday • I Saw Mommy Kissing Santa Claus • I'll Be Home for Christmas • Let It Snow! Let It Snow! Let It Snow! • Little Saint Nick • Snowfall.

VOL. 32 – THE OFFSPRING 00699653 / $14.95
Bad Habit • Come Out and Play • Gone Away • Gotta Get Away • Hit That • The Kids Aren't Alright • Pretty Fly (For a White Guy) • Self Esteem.

VOL. 33 – ACOUSTIC CLASSICS 00699656 / $12.95
Across the Universe • Babe, I'm Gonna Leave You • Crazy on You • Heart of Gold • Hotel California • I'd Love to Change the World • Thick As a Brick • Wanted Dead or Alive.

VOL. 34 – CLASSIC ROCK 00699658 / $12.95
Aqualung • Born to Be Wild • The Boys Are Back in Town • Brown Eyed Girl • Reeling in the Years • Rock'n Me • Rocky Mountain Way • Sweet Emotion.

VOL. 35 – HAIR METAL 00699660 / $12.95
Decadence Dance • Don't Treat Me Bad • Down Boys • Seventeen • Shake Me • Up All Night • Wait • Your Mama Don't Dance.

VOL. 36 – SOUTHERN ROCK 00699661 / $12.95
Can't You See • Flirtin' with Disaster • Hold on Loosely • Jessica • Mississippi Queen • Ramblin' Man • Sweet Home Alabama • What's Your Name.

VOL. 37 – ACOUSTIC METAL 00699662 / $12.95
Every Rose Has Its Thorn • Fly to the Angels • Hole Hearted • I'll Never Let You Go • Love Is on the Way • Love of a Lifetime • To Be with You • When the Children Cry.

VOL. 38 – BLUES 00699663 / $12.95
As the Years Go Passing By • Boom Boom • Cold Shot • Everyday I Have the Blues • Frosty • Further On up the Road • Killing Floor • Texas Flood.

VOL. 39 – '80S METAL 00699664 / $12.95
Bark at the Moon • Big City Nights • Breaking the Chains • Cult of Personality • Lay It Down • Living on a Prayer • Panama • Smokin' in the Boys Room.

VOL. 40 – INCUBUS 00699668 / $14.95
Are You In? • Drive • Megalomaniac • Nice to Know You • Pardon Me • Stellar • Talk Shows on Mute • Wish You Were Here.

VOL. 41 – ERIC CLAPTON 00699669 / $14.95
After Midnight • Can't Find My Way Home • Forever Man • I Shot the Sheriff • I'm Tore Down • Pretending • Running on Faith • Tears in Heaven.

VOL. 42 – CHART HITS 00699670 / $12.95
Are You Gonna Be My Girl • Heaven • Here Without You • I Believe in a Thing Called Love • Just Like You • Last Train Home • This Love • Until the Day I Die.

VOL. 43 – LYNYRD SKYNYRD 00699681 / $14.95
Don't Ask Me No Questions • Free Bird • Gimme Three Steps • I Know a Little • Saturday Night Special • Sweet Home Alabama • That Smell • You Got That Right.

Prices, contents, and availability subject to change without notice.

FOR MORE INFORMATION, SEE YOUR LOCAL MUSIC DEALER, OR WRITE TO:

HAL•LEONARD® CORPORATION
7777 W. BLUEMOUND RD. P.O. BOX 13819 MILWAUKEE, WI 53213

Visit Hal Leonard online at www.halleonard.com

0305